D0597554

LANGUAGE!®

The Comprehensive Literacy Curriculum

Jane Fell Greene, Ed.D.

SOPRIS WEST EDUCATIONAL SERVICES
A CAMBIUM LEARNING COMPANY

BOSTON, MA • NEW YORK, NY • LONGMONT, CO

10 09 08 07   12 11 10 9 8 7 6

Editorial Director: Nancy Chapel Eberhardt
Word and Phrase Selection: Judy Fell Woods
English Learners: Jennifer Wells Greene
Lesson Development: Sheryl Ferlito, Donna Lutz
Morphology: John Alexander, Mike Minsky, Bruce Rosow
Text Selection: Sara Buckerfield, Jim Cloonan
Decodable Text: Jenny Hamilton, Steve Harmon

LANGUAGE! eReader is a customized version of the
CAST eReader for Windows® (3.0). CAST eReader
©1995—2003, CAST, Inc. and its licensors. All rights reserved.

ISBN 1-59318-262-7

Printed in the United States of America

Published and distributed by

Sopris West™
EDUCATIONAL SERVICES

A Cambium Learning Company

4093 Specialty Place • Longmont, CO 80504 • (303) 651-2829
www.sopriswest.com

70287/2-07

"What we play is life."

—Louis Armstrong (1900–1971)

Table of Contents

This book contains six units.

Each unit builds knowledge in:

- Sounds and Letters
- Spelling and Words
- Vocabulary and Roots
- Grammar and Usage
- Listening and Reading
- Speaking and Writing

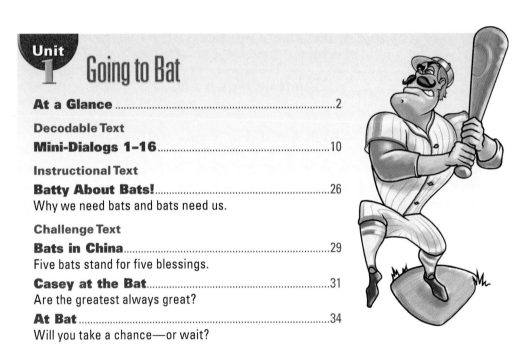

Unit 4 Twins Together

Appendix

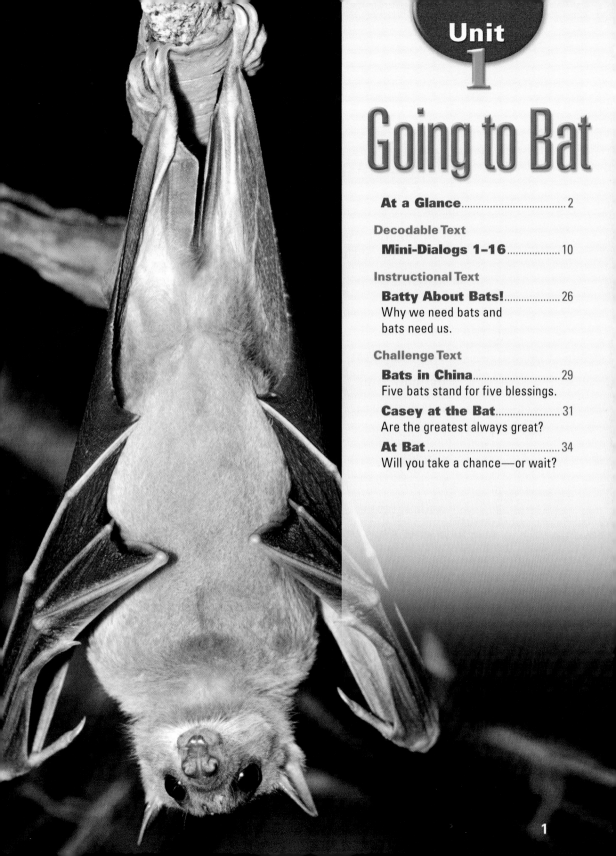

Unit 1

Going to Bat

1

STEP
1

Phonemic Awareness and Phonics

Languages have two kinds of sounds: **consonants** and **vowels**.

- Consonants are closed sounds. They restrict or close the airflow using the lips, teeth, or tongue.
- Vowels are open sounds. They keep the airflow open.

Unit 1 has six consonant sounds and one vowel sound. Letters represent the sounds.

- **Consonants:**

  m (mat, bam)

  s (sat, cats)

  t (tam, mat)

  c (cat)

  f (fat)

  b (bat, tab)

  The letter **s** has two sounds: / s / (sat, cats) and / z / (cabs).

Go to the **Consonant Chart** on page 209. Find the sounds for these letters: **m**, **s**, **t**, **c**, **f**, and **b**.

- **Vowel:** The vowel is short / a / spelled **a** (at, pan, glad).

Go to the **Vowel Chart** on page 210. Find ă for short / a /. Find the example word **cat**.

STEP

2 Word Recognition and Spelling

We put vowels and consonants together to make words. Every English word has at least one vowel.

Two English words are made of just one vowel. They are **I** and **a**. All other English words combine consonants and vowels.

> **Examples: Unit Words**
> **at**, **mat**, **mast**

We use some words often in everything we say, read, or write. These are called:

Essential Words

a, are, I, is, that, the, this

Spelling Lists: The Unit 1 spelling lists contain two word categories:

1. Words with these six consonants <u>m</u>, <u>s</u>, <u>t</u>, <u>c</u>, <u>f</u>, and <u>b</u> and short / *a* / spelled <u>a</u>

2. **Essential Words** (in italics)

Spelling Lists			
Lessons 1—5		**Lessons 6—10**	
a	sat	act	cab
are	tab	am	cat
fat	*that*	as	fact
I	*the*	at	fast
is	*this*	bat	tact

Vocabulary and Morphology

Unit Vocabulary: Sound-spelling correspondences from this unit make up this unit's vocabulary.

- ■ What do these words mean?
- ■ Do some of them mean more than one thing? Which ones?

UNIT Vocabulary

m, s, t, c, f, b, a for short /a/

act	bat	fast
am	cat	fat
at	fact	sat

Meaning Parts: Adding certain letters to words can add to or change their meanings. Many words mean "one of something." **Singular** means "one of something."

Example: Singular
The word **bat** means one **bat**.

Adding **-s** changes the word to mean "more than one." **Plural** means "more than one."

Example: Plural
Bats can mean more than one **bat**.

Grammar and Usage

In English, words have different functions (jobs). Sometimes the same word can have two functions. Look at the nouns and verbs in these boxes.

Nouns name people, places, or things. Read these Unit 1 nouns.

- Which ones are things?
- Are there any people or places on this list?

Nouns

act	cast	fat	scab
bat	cat	mast	tab
cab	fact	mat	

Verbs describe actions. Read these Unit 1 verbs.

Verbs

act	bat	cast	sat	tab

Sentences convey a complete thought by answering two questions: Who (or what) did it? and What did they (he, she, or it) do? In English, we put nouns and verbs together to make sentences.

Example: Sentence

What did it?	cat (noun)
What did it do?	sat (verb)
The complete thought:	The cat sat. (sentence)

This sentence pattern is N/V. The diagram below shows how to build the sentence.

N/V   noun/verb

The cat sat. (*noun / action verb*)

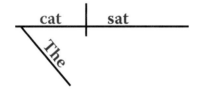

STEP

5

Listening and Reading

We read different types of text.

- Some text provides information. In informational text, we listen and read for the topic and details that support that topic. Details include ideas and facts.

- Some text tells a story. When we read a story, we listen or look for the parts of a story: characters, setting, events, and resolution.

Knowing the kind of text helps us focus on the right kind of information. When we focus on the right kind of information, we understand the text.

STEP

6 Speaking and Writing

We use different types of sentences when we speak and write.

Some sentences tell something. These are called statements.

> **Examples: Statements**
>
> **The cab is fast.** This tells us something about the cab.
>   What? It is fast.
>
> **Sam can act.** This tells us something Sam can do.
>   What? He can act.

Some sentences ask for information. These are called questions.

> **Examples: Questions**
>
> **Is the bat fat?** This asks us something about the way the bat looks.
>
>   How does it look? The bat is fat.
>
> **Is Sam in the cab?** This asks us something about where Sam is.
>
>   Where is he? He is in the cab.

More About Words

Expand vocabulary by learning these Bonus Words. Bonus Words are more words composed of the sound-spelling correspondences that we have studied in this unit.

UNIT Bonus Words

ab	cast	scab	stab
bam	mast	scam	tab
cab	mat	scat	tact

Why? Word History

Letter a—The Anglo-Saxons used the Roman alphabet to write their language. But the Old English language had some sounds (phonemes) that Latin did not have. One of those sounds was the sound we call short / a /. They used the symbol **æ** to write the sound. Today, we just use the letter **a**.

Stage Setting

Mac and his friend are alley cats. They live on the streets. They're tough.

Critic's Corner

1. What do Mac and his friend think of Samantha (Sam), the actress?

2. Why would Mac say that Sam is "**not** a cat"?

Stage Setting

It's late at night. Bats are out, flying and feeding. The theater has just closed.

Critic's Corner

1. What do the bats think of Sam?

2. What does Sam think of the bats?

Critic's Corner

1. The painting is abstract. What do you think the term *abstract art* means?

2. Do you think these people really like the painting?

Stage Setting

In the art gallery, we can learn as much about people as we can about art.

Critic's Corner

1. Abstract art can be just line and color, a picture of an idea. People want to see a thing. Why do people search for a thing in paintings?

2. Do these two people really enjoy the art?

Stage Setting

At a baseball stadium, the players are getting ready to play an important game.

Critic's Corner

1. The baseball players worry about the bats they are choosing. Are the bats really that different?

2. Why do you think the players spend so much time and effort choosing the bats?

Stage Setting

In a gym, observing workouts, we can learn much about ourselves and others.

Critic's Corner

1. How are the two bats in the gym like people?

2. How are the two bats alike? How are they different? At the end of their workouts, why would they say, "I am bats!"?

Stage Setting

People's personalities can be strong—and different. The same thing is true of animals. Imagine the cat conversation below.

Critic's Corner

1. Do people ever act this way?

2. Besides humans, what other animals might compare their talents or their looks?

Stage Setting

Samantha (Sam) *seems* to have lots of confidence. She's getting ready to go on stage.

Critic's Corner

1. What does the dialog above tell you about Samantha, the cat?

2. Is Samantha convinced that she can act?

Stage Setting

Casey is a super-athlete. People go to a game just to see Casey.

Critic's Corner

1. Why do you think people love super-athletes?

2. Who is your favorite athlete? Why?

Mini-Dialog 10

Stage Setting
Casey comes up to bat. Everyone wonders what will happen.

Critic's Corner

1. Casey is a super-athlete. Do you think the announcer makes him nervous?

2. Is Casey able to concentrate on what he is doing? Explain why.

Stage Setting

Super-athletes don't have much privacy. Casey is trying to go somewhere without being noticed.

Critic's Corner

1. Lots of people dream about becoming famous. Do you think Casey enjoys being famous?

2. How would you feel if you always had people watching you and judging you?

Stage Setting

The restaurant is advertising *Free Food*. That sounds too good to be true. Maybe there is a catch.

Critic's Corner

1. Are the people really paying for the food? How?

2. What does *scam* mean? Do you think this is a scam? Why?

Stage Setting

Samantha loves acting in the cast. Tonight, she lets some others act with her.

Critic's Corner

1. Samantha is a great actress. Why does it take a whole cast, and not just one actor or actress, to create a good play or movie?

2. What do you think the cast members think of Samantha? Why?

Mini-Dialog 14

Stage Setting

The play has ended, and the cast is leaving. They had a great time at the play.

Critic's Corner

1. The cast members have been working together. Now they want to go out together. Why do they like being together?

2. Why do you think they want to squeeze into the cab together?

Stage Setting
Samantha has had an accident. She is not feeling well.

Critic's Corner

1. What do you think happened to Samantha?

2. Why do we visit people who have been hurt or who are sick?

Stage Setting

Sam and Mac have become friends. She's even agreed to go fishing with him.

Critic's Corner

1. Sam is still in a cast from her accident. How is Mac helping her?

2. When she no longer needs help, will she and Mac still be friends? Why do you think so?

Batty About Bats!

Flying and Feeding

mammals
warm-blooded animals

Do **mammals** fly? One can fly. Which one? The bat can fly. Bats have an extra skin. It is thin. This skin connects parts of the bat. It joins its hands, arms, and ankles. The skin makes wings. Bats use the wings to fly.
5 They fly at night. They look for food. They need their wings to eat.

Bats eat a lot. Flying takes energy. Food makes energy. Bats eat half their weight each day! They eat at night. Bats eat a lot of things. Some eat fruits. Some eat flowers.
10 Some eat frogs and fish. Some eat lizards. Some eat bugs. They eat mosquitoes. They eat flies. They eat moths. They even eat termites!

Super Sonar

sonar
use of sound waves to locate objects; echolocation

Did you think bats were blind? They are not. They see. Some have good vision. Bats fly at night. It is dark.
15 Can they see? Yes! They use sonar to "see."

Bats can "hear" where they are. They use echoes. Bats can "see" with sound. They cry out. The sound comes back. It echoes. We can't hear these sounds. But bats can. Bats use other clues, too. Bugs buzz around. Bats hear
20 them. Lots of bugs mean lots of food.

The Marianas flying fox eats fruit.

Hanging Out and Helping

Bats hang. They hang upside down. They hang when they sleep. Bats live in trees. Bats live in buildings. Bats live in caves. Many live in one cave. These are **bat colonies** .

25 Bats "go to bat" for the Earth. They eat a lot of bugs. Bats save plants. Bugs kill plants. Farmers can lose their farms. Millions would be hungry.

Bats help plants. They scatter seeds. Think about this. There is a fruit in Asia. It makes millions in cash.
30 What if there were no bats? This plant could not grow. It could not spread. Farmers would lose the fruit. They would lose the cash.

bat colonies
large groups of bats living together

Bats in Trouble

Today, bats are in danger. People hurt their homes. We **interfere** in their colonies. We use chemicals.
35 There are plans. The plans help bats. One plan shuts gates to old mines. This keeps people out. But it lets bats in. Some chemicals kill bats. One plan stops them. These plans help everyone.

interfere
to hinder or disrupt; impede

A vampire bat goes for a "walk."

All photos © Merlin D. Tuttle Bat Conservation Intl.

Scientists teach us about bats. Others help bats live.
40 They count bat colonies. They study bats. What can you do for bats?

"There is no point in finding out more about these fascinating creatures if we destroy them with **ignorance** and **negligence**," says one expert. "Bats
45 need friends!"

Adapted from "Batty About Bats!"
by Kathiann M. Kowalski

ignorance
uninformed or unaware

negligence
habitual careless-ness or irresponsi-bility

Answer It
Say the answer in a complete sentence.
See question 1.

1. Is a bat a mammal?
   Answer: Yes, a bat is a mammal.

2. Are all bats bug-eaters?

3. Are bats blind?

4. Are bats able to "see" with sound?

5. Do bats sleep standing up?

6. Do bats eat at night?

7. Do bats live in cages?

8. Are bats dangerous to farmers?

9. Are bats helpful to crops?

10. Are bats in danger?

Bats in China

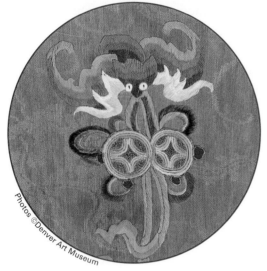

A woman's informal robe, China, 1875-1900, is decorated with red bats. Photo by William O'Conner, Denver Art Museum.

Photos ©Denver Art Museum

In one **culture**, something is **honored**. In another culture, it may be despised. Western people detest bats. In Europe and in early America, bats suggested demons and evil. In the East, it is the opposite. In much of Asia,
5   bats are **prized**.

Chinese culture is thousands of years old. The Chinese have always prized bats. The Chinese word for bat is *fu* (pronounced *foo*). It sounds like their word for luck, *fu*. Thousands of years ago, the Chinese thought
10   about the world. They looked for balance. They tried to find balance in life. They searched for balance of strong and weak. They valued balance between male

culture
the language, customs, and beliefs of a group of people

honored
respected, admired

prized
treasured, valued

and female. The bat was a male sign. Flowers and fruits were female signs.

15   In China bats have been common in art. The Chinese decorated with bats. They embroidered bats on clothing. They painted bats on dishes. They carved bats. They displayed them in their homes. This brought happiness and long life. In their **shrines**, the Chinese

20   used bats to honor their dead.

Bats are often red, the color of happiness. A group of five bats shows that someone has lived a good life. The five bats stand for five blessings. They are: health; long life; **prosperity**; love of **virtue**; and a peaceful,

25   natural death. Sometimes, it is hard to see the art bats. They may look more like flowers or leaves.

Bats live to be very old. They live much longer than any other small mammal. We do not know why. We do know this. In China, bats mean wisdom and old age.

30   May you have many bats!

shrines
sacred or spiritual places

prosperity
financial success

virtue
moral excellence, goodness

These Chinese characters for fu *mean* "bat."

Think About It

1. In Chinese, what does the word *fu* mean? Does it mean more than one thing?

2. Five bats stand for five blessings. What are they?

3. What did you learn about the life span of bats?

4. Why do you think Europeans revile, which means strongly dislike, bats?

5. Why do you think Asians revere, which means worship or honor, bats?

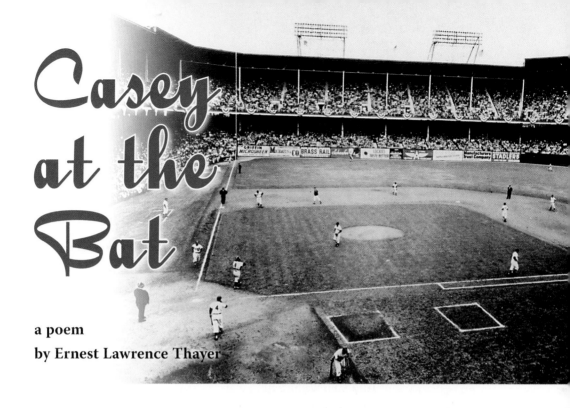

Casey at the Bat

a poem

by Ernest Lawrence Thayer

Summary: Casey was a **legendary** baseball player in the 1800s. He played for the Mudville team. The fans called him "Mighty Casey." This was because he always hit the ball so hard, and so far. He was a star!

5 Before television, lots of people went to baseball games in the summer. A **famous** poem, "Casey at the Bat," tells the story of one special game.

This was the most important game of the season. The score was 4 to 2, and Mudville was behind. The
10 fans could only hope that Casey would get up to bat. If he did, they knew he could win it for Mudville! But there was little hope that Casey would get up to bat. The game was in the last inning. Mudville was behind. The 5,000 fans were losing hope.

15 But the two batters ahead of Casey got hits, and the bases were loaded! With three on base, Mighty Casey took his place at home plate. All the fans counted on him, because he was their star. Casey was ready to win for Mudville. Everybody knew he would pull through.
20 With the first two pitches, Casey made two **strikes** .

legendary
extremely well-known; mythical

famous
having widespread recognition

strikes
failure to hit pitched balls

These last lines of the poem tell you what happened next:

stern

grim, uninviting

They saw his face grow **stern** and cold; they saw his
    muscles strain,
And they knew that Casey wouldn't let that ball go by again.

sneer

a disrespectful
smile; smirk

The **sneer** is gone from Casey's lip; his teeth are clenched
5   in hate;
He pounds with cruel violence his bat upon the plate.
And now the pitcher holds the ball and now he lets it go,
And now the air is shattered by the force of Casey's blow.

Oh! Somewhere in this favored land the
10   sun is shining bright;
The band is playing somewhere, and
    somewhere hearts are light,
And somewhere men are
    laughing, and somewhere
15   children shout;
But there is no joy in
    Mudville—Mighty
    Casey has struck out.

Think About It

1. Have you ever thought that lots of people were counting on you? How does it feel?

2. What was the name of the team that Casey played for?

3. The fans called him "Mighty Casey." How did he get that name?

4. "They saw his face grow stern and cold . . ." Why would Casey have this kind of look on his face?

5. In the last stanza (the last 10 lines), the poem creates contrast. What is the contrast between the first seven lines and the last three lines in the stanza?

6. Why do you think the poet used this contrast?

At Bat

by Jacqueline Hechtkopf

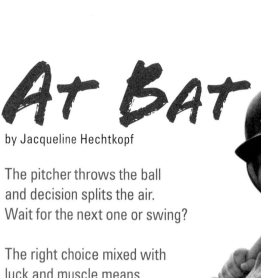

The pitcher throws the ball
and decision splits the air.
Wait for the next one or swing?

The right choice mixed with
5   luck and muscle means
the crowd will stand
and cheer.

Forget wrong decisions
returning in silence
10 to sulk on the bench.

That was last time
and the time before.

Keep your eye on the ball
and send fear sailing
15 over the fence.

Think About It

1. Everybody has made poor choices. Everybody has made bad decisions. When we do, we can choose again: try once more or "sulk on the bench." What does the poet really mean by "sulk on the bench"?

2. What is the poet recommending here?

3. Is there a way to know if we are making the "right choice"?

4. Are we able to forget what has happened in the past? What will happen to our future if we always let the past control our decisions?

5. Can you think of how this advice might help you? How it might help someone you know?

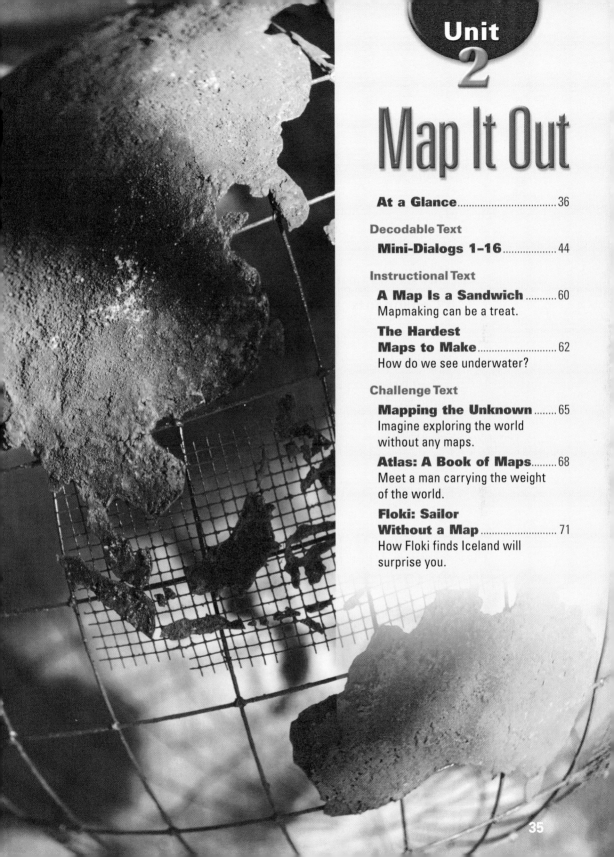

Unit
2
Map It Out

STEP
1

■ Phonemic Awareness and Phonics

One type of speech sound is a **consonant**. Consonants are closed sounds. They restrict or close the airflow with lips, teeth, or tongue.

Unit 2 has six consonant sounds. Letters represent the sounds.

■ **Consonants:**

n (nap, tan)

l (lab, pal)

h (hat)

r (rat)

j (jam)

p (pat, tap)

Review: The letter **s** represents two sounds: / s / (sat, cats) and / z / (cabs).

Go to the **Consonant Chart** on page 209. Find the sounds for these letters: **n**, **l**, **h**, **r**, **j**, and **p**.

Word Recognition and Spelling

We put consonants and vowels together to make words. Every English word has at least one vowel.

> **Examples: Unit Words**
>
> **an, map, ramp**

We use some words often in everything we say, read, or write. These words are called:

Essential Words

do, said, to, who, you, your

Spelling Lists: The Unit 2 spelling lists contain two word categories:

1. Words with the six new consonants **n**, **l**, **h**, **r**, **j**, **p** and short / *a* / spelled **a**

2. **Essential Words** (in italics)

Spelling Lists			
Lessons 1–5		**Lessons 6–10**	
can	*said*	an	lamp
do	*to*	asp	last
has	*who*	cap	plant
man	*you*	clap	raft
map	*your*	flat	strap

Vocabulary and Morphology

Unit Vocabulary: Sound-spelling correspondences from this and the previous unit make up this unit's vocabulary.

- What do these words mean?

- Do some of them mean more than one thing? Which ones?

UNIT Vocabulary

n, l, h, r, j, p

abstract	clap	jam	past	scalp
an	fan	lamp	pat	slam
ant	flap	last	plan	slap
as	flat	man	plant	strap
blast	ham	map	ran	tan
can	has	nap	rat	tap
cap	hat	pan	sap	trap

Antonyms: Antonyms have opposite meanings.
Example: above/below; dead/alive; happy/sad.

- Think of opposites for the **Unit Vocabulary** words.

Meaning Parts: Adding letters or punctuation to words can add to or change their meanings. Adding **'s** signals singular possession. This means that one person or thing owns something.

Examples: Singular Possession

The **man's map** means the map that belongs to the man.

One man owns one map.

Fran's stamps means the stamps that belong to Fran.

A person, Fran, owns several stamps.

The **cab's mats** means the mats that belong to the cab.

A thing, the cab, possesses mats.

STEP 4

Grammar and Usage

Nouns have several functions (jobs). Nouns serve as the subjects of sentences.

- The **subject** is one of two main parts of English sentences.
- The **subject** names the person, place, or thing that the sentence is about.

Read these Unit 2 nouns. They can be the subjects of sentences.

Nouns

ant	craft	man	rat
asp	fan	map	sap
blast	flap	nap	scalp
can	flat	pact	slab
cap	ham	pal	stamp
camp	hat	pan	strap
clam	jam	plan	tract
clamp	lab	plant	tramp
crab	lamp	raft	trap

In English, nouns show possession through the use of **'s**
Sam's map refers to the map that belongs to Sam.

The **predicate** is the second of the two main parts of English sentences.

- The **predicate** contains the main verb of the sentence.
- The **predicate** usually comes after the subject.

Read these Unit 2 verbs. They can be the predicates of sentences.

Verbs

blast	nap	rap	stamp
can	pant	scan	strap
clamp	plan	scrap	tap
clap	plant	slam	tramp
fan	ram	slap	trap
flap	ran	snap	
map	rant	span	

A **simple sentence** has one subject and one predicate.

- The subject answers: "Who (or what) did it?"
- The predicate answers: "What did they (he, she, or it) do?"

> **Example: Simple Sentence**
>
> **The man ran.**
>> Who did it? The man
>> What did he do? ran

The following diagram shows how to build this sentence with a subject and predicate.

N/V   **noun/verb**

S/P   **subject/predicate**

The man ran. (*subject / predicate*)

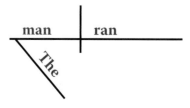

Listening and Reading Comprehension

We read different types of text.

- Some text provides information. In informational text, we listen and read for the topic and details that support that topic. Details include ideas and facts.

- Some text tells a story. When we read a story, we listen or look for the parts of a story: characters, setting, events, and resolution.

Knowing the kind of text helps us focus on the right kind of information. When we focus on the right kind of information, we understand the text.

STEP

6

Speaking and Writing

We use different types of sentences when we speak and write.

Some sentences tell something. These are called statements.

> **Examples: Statements**
>
> **The plan is abstract.** This tells us something about the plan.
> What? It is abstract.
>
> **The man ran.** This tells us something the man did.
> What? He ran.
>
> **This is your map.** This tells us something about the map.
> What? It is your map.

Some sentences ask for information. These are called questions. Questions beginning with **who** require answers that name a person or group of people.

> **Examples: Questions**
>
> **Who has the map?** The man has the map.
> *Man* tells **who** has the map.
>
> **Who is in the cast?** Sam is in the cast.
> *Sam* tells **who** is in the cast.
>
> **Who is in the cab?** The cast is in the cab.
> *The cast* tells **who** is in the cab.

More About Words

Expand vocabulary by learning these Bonus Words. Bonus Words use the sound-spelling correspondences that we have studied in this unit and previous units.

UNIT Bonus Words

aft	camp	lab	ramp	snap
alp	clam	lap	rant	span
amp	clamp	nab	rap	spat
asp	clasp	pact	scan	stamp
ban	crab	pal	scrap	stat
blab	craft	pant	slab	tract
bran	cram	raft	slant	tramp
brat	flab	ram	slat	

Why? Word History

Apostrophe—A long time ago, English people wrote "man's hat" as "mannes hat." The suffix **-es** showed ownership. At that time, people pronounced the <u>e</u>. Today we show possession with **'s**.

Stage Setting

People need maps for lots of things. This sailor needs an ocean map. An ocean map looks different from a land map.

Critic's Corner

1. If the parrot has the sailor's map, how will the sailor find his way?

2. Discuss this statement: *A map is more important at sea than it is on land.* Do you agree or disagree? Why?

Stage Setting

Two scientists have just arrived at the airport and gotten into a cab. They are headed to an important meeting at a science lab in a large city.

Critic's Corner

1. These scientists can understand all kinds of difficult ideas and they have a lot to think about. Why did they forget the map to the lab?

2. Have you ever forgotten something important when you were busy?

Stage Setting

Sometimes, we are misled. See how easily these aliens are misled.

Critic's Corner

1. What confused the aliens?

2. What would have happened if they had a globe instead of a map?

Stage Setting

When we don't have information about a subject, we can draw the wrong conclusion. These aliens seem to have drawn the wrong conclusion.

Critic's Corner

1. Why did the aliens conclude that the CAT scan was a diagnostic machine for cats?

2. What does CAT scan (sometimes called CT scan) stand for?

Mini-Dialog 5

Stage Setting

It's a good thing to try to appreciate the work of a sculptor. Sometimes, abstract sculpture is difficult to understand if you do not know the sculptor's intent.

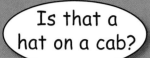

Critic's Corner

1. These people were trying to understand the sculptor's work. What might have made it easier for them to understand the sculptor's work?

2. Is it hard to understand art? Why?

Stage Setting

Paintings can be abstract, and artists may require us to think about what we are seeing. Abstract art is interesting because different people see different things in the same painting.

Critic's Corner

1. Compare and contrast representational (realistic) art and abstract art. How are they alike? How are they different?

2. Which do you prefer? Why?

Stage Setting

Like people, animals have different kinds of talent. Some are more athletic than others. Some are super-runners.

Critic's Corner

1. The people are amazed by the dog's running ability. Have you ever known an animal that had some special talent?

2. Describe the special abilities of some animals.

Stage Setting

Sometimes, we get into contests that are silly. Think about the following competition and why it is silly.

Critic's Corner

1. Have you ever felt like you were competing out of your league? What put you in that position?

2. In school, is there a subject that is easier for you than for others?

Stage Setting

Life sometimes offers us the unexpected. Usually, we're not ready to handle it, because we didn't see it coming.

Critic's Corner

1. The fisherman didn't get the crabs he was fishing for. Was he upset?

2. What do you expect the fisherman to do next?

Stage Setting

We all have fears. Sometimes, our fears are unreasonable.

Critic's Corner

1. Maybe elephants aren't really afraid of ants. But they do have fears. Explain why we sometimes have unreasonable fears.

2. Remember when you were a small child. Think of some unreasonable fear that you had. Why do you think you feared it?

Stage Setting

Everybody should have healthy fears. These scientists realize the danger they have encountered.

Critic's Corner

1. Can we ever feel 100 percent safe?

2. Think of three professions that require healthy fear. What is the difference between a healthy fear and an unhealthy fear?

Stage Setting

Sometimes, we use the wrong tool to do a job. Sometimes, we expect others to do the impossible.

Critic's Corner

1. Sometimes, we try to do a job without the right tools. Think of a situation when something has failed because the right tools weren't used.

2. Can we think of people's talents as tools?

Stage Setting

Each of us has different interests. It's always good to find others who share our interests.

Critic's Corner

1. These people share the interest of acting. What interest would you like to pursue?

2. Give three reasons for your interest. How could you pursue your interest?

Stage Setting
Of course, there are no genies, but old stories said that genies could grant special wishes.

Critic's Corner

1. Why do you think the alien was happy to go to the past?

2. Is there a time in the past that you would like to visit?

Stage Setting

There are thousands of strange animals that people seldom see. Zoos are wonderful places, as long as the animals are well cared for. But this space zoo is weird.

Critic's Corner

1. The aliens are visiting a zoo unlike any on Earth. What is different about their space zoo?

2. Are you aware of any creatures on Earth that are as bizarre as these creatures?

Stage Setting

Even aliens find unusual creatures in the space zoo. Think about what causes their surprise.

> Is that a bat in pants?

> Yes. And that asp naps on a raft.

> Look! The clams are in a cab!

> This is a blast!

Critic's Corner

1. What do the aliens find unusual about the animals in the space zoo?

2. Comedy writers for TV, movies, and books have to think about what makes a situation funny. What do you think turns an ordinary situation into a comedy?

A Map Is a Sandwich

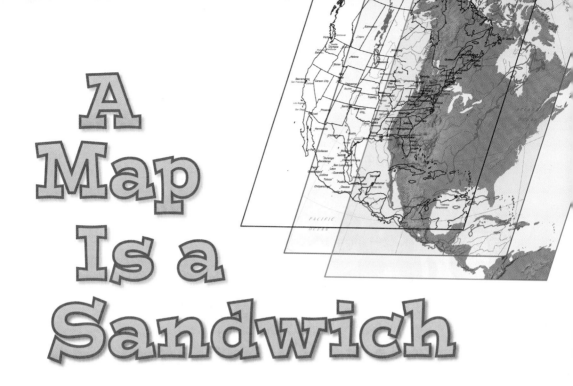

Making a map is like making a sandwich. Think about it. A sandwich has layers. First, there is a layer of bread. Then, there is a layer of mustard. Add lettuce. Next, add meat. Then add a layer of cheese. Last, add
5 more bread.

Stacy and Diana are cartographers. They make maps. They need facts. They use facts from the sky. They get facts from land. Facts come from **satellites**. Facts come from **surveys**. Pictures of lines come to
10 them. Diana and Stacy turn the lines into maps.

First, they study the lines. The lines show rivers. They show roads. Stacy and Diana ask questions. What lines are **borders**? What lines are roads? What lines are rivers? What lines are forests?

15 Stacy explains. "We make maps. We work in layers. We begin with the lines. They give us layers of information. It's like making a sandwich. Say you're making a map. How do you start? With a layer of land. You'd add a layer of forest. Add the rivers. Add the
20 roads. And the last layer? Names of cities and towns."

satellites
information-gathering spacecraft

surveys
studies of land features using special tools and formulas

borders
dividing lines between specific areas

Next, they add color. Diana tells why. "Important things have to stand out. They need bright colors. Making a map of state parks? Show the parks in bright green."

Last, they make a **key**. The key shows symbols.
25 It uses colors. A tiny tent is a campground. A tiny airplane is an airport. Major highways are **bold** red lines. A small road is a row of dashes. The key shows what the symbols mean. When the key is easy to understand, the map is good. Stacy explains, "You want
30 everybody to understand it. Not everybody is good with maps. When is a map *really* good? When you don't have to look at the key!"

"No map is perfect," Stacy says. "There is a big problem. Maps are flat. But the Earth is round." Stacy is
35 right. Maps have **limits**. But without them, we'd be lost!

Adapted from "A Map Is a Sandwich" by Jeanne Miller

key
a table of information on a map

bold
noticeably darkened

limits
weaknesses or shortcomings

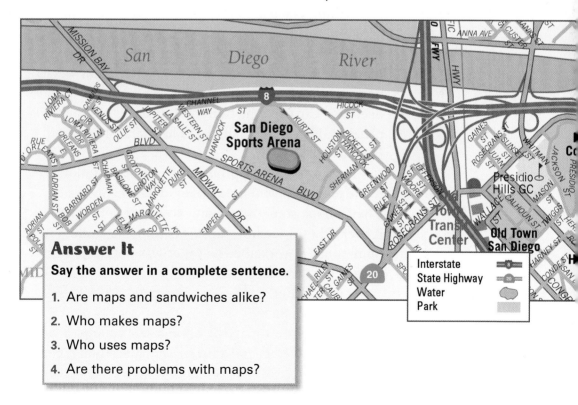

Answer It

Say the answer in a complete sentence.

1. Are maps and sandwiches alike?

2. Who makes maps?

3. Who uses maps?

4. Are there problems with maps?

Interstate
State Highway
Water
Park

The Hardest Maps to Make

A Hard Job

Making maps is fun. We can see land. We can map it. We can map mountains. We can map **plains**. We can map valleys. But how about water? Can we map water— **ponds**, **lakes**, and **rivers**? Can we
5 map oceans? Oceans are the hardest to map. They are deep. We can't see the bottom. It is dark. We can't take pictures. Fish can't talk to us. They can't share their travels.

This is an ancient problem. In old days, sailors
10 made maps. They mapped lakes. They mapped seas. They'd hook something heavy to a rope. They'd drop it over. They'd see how far it was to the bottom. Sometimes it worked if the water was not deep. But oceans are very deep!

Mapping With Sonar

15 Sonar helps us map the oceans. We couldn't map deep water. We needed a better way. We studied bats.

plains
large, flat, treeless areas of land

ponds
small bodies of still water

lakes
large bodies of still water

rivers
large streams of flowing water

Bats helped mapmakers. Bats "see" in the dark. They use sound to "see." They use echoes.

Sonar is a "sound camera." Sonar doesn't use light. 20 It uses sound. It counts distance. It counts the time for sound to come back. (Just like bats!) Echoes sound different. Deep places sound different than shallow places. The computer helps. It turns sounds into pictures! The pictures show the bottom.

25 But sonar is not perfect. It is slow. We have worked for 50 years. Only parts of the oceans are mapped. What if we use the best sonar? It would still take over 100 years. The ocean is 70 percent of the Earth's surface! There is another problem. It is cost. Sonar costs a lot.

©E. Paul Oberlander, Woods Hole Oceanographic Institution

Ocean Mapping Today

30   In 1997, scientists had an idea. They used two things. They used sound. They used satellites. They used them *together.* They took pictures of land. They took pictures of water. These were more accurate. Today ocean maps are better. We have new vehicles. They work on the ocean
35 floor. They don't need people. They take pictures of the ocean floor.

frontier

an undeveloped area of exploration

Mapping Earth's Last Frontier

The oceans are huge. They cover many miles. Maps will take years to finish. It is important work. We must get it done. These maps help us find fish. They help
40 us find minerals. They measure the ocean's flow. That flow **affects** our weather. It affects shipping. It affects trade. It affects travel. These maps give facts we need. The ocean is the last frontier for mapmakers.

affects

causes a change in; influences

Answer It
Say the answer in a complete sentence.

1. Who learned about using sound and echoes from bats?

2. Sonar is a "sound camera." What does that mean?

3. Are there limits with sonar?

4. What has improved ocean mapping since 1997?

5. Explain the last sentence: The ocean is the last frontier for mapmakers.

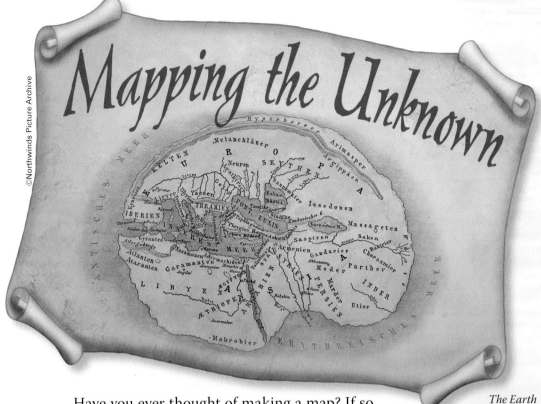

Mapping the Unknown

The Earth according to Herodotus.

Have you ever thought of making a map? If so, how would you begin? Stand at your front door. Try to draw a map of your block. It is hard. You can't see the whole block. Today, maps are exact. We use pictures
5 from airplanes. We use pictures from satellites. But making maps has not always been easy.

Early mapmakers had to trust what they could see. They had to talk to travelers. They learned from explorers. A traveler might say that a city lay where a
10 river flowed into the sea. Sailors might tell of islands off a coast. Maybe they recalled a bay near some cliffs. Mapmakers drew these on their maps.

Early mapmakers had to judge the distance between places. They learned how long it took to go from one
15 place to another. Travelers would tell how much time they had spent on their trips. Mapmakers learned how long it took to walk. They learned how long it took by horse. They counted how many days it took by ship.

The first mapmakers used the sun and stars to map
20 places far away. Was the place in the East, where the sun rises? Or was it in the West, where the sun sets?

Sailors knew about the winds. They told of winds that blew from the north. These winds pushed ships toward islands in the south. They told of winds from the east
25 that took them to a western shore.

Early maps were full of mistakes. There were no satellites. There were no airplanes. There was no way to take pictures from the sky. Judging distance was a big problem. For example, **Columbus** believed the world
30 was much smaller. In 1492, he sailed west. He landed on an island. He thought he was in Asia. But Asia was thousands of miles farther away!

Sometimes, travelers misled mapmakers. Some told of a land bridge between southern Africa and southeastern
35 Asia. Others said the Americas were one **continent** . Some maps showed places as explorers hoped they would be. For example, they showed a sea passage to China through North America. Of course, no such passage exists.

40 Travelers also told of creatures they had seen. Sometimes they **exaggerated** . Whales became "sea monsters." Lizards and snakes became " **dragons** ." These fantastic creatures were **intriguing** . Mapmakers added them to their maps.

45 People feared the unknown. What lay beyond the mountains? What was at the edge of the sea? Perhaps there *were* dragons! Mapmakers had to include unexplored land and seas. They often used dragons and sea monsters on their maps. These **indicated** the
50 unknown.

Today, we have airplanes and satellites. We have filled in the mysterious spaces. What is left to map? The bottoms of the oceans are not completely mapped. Do you think there are dragons down there?

Columbus
famous Italian explorer

continent
a major landmass

exaggerated
overstated or magnified

dragons
mythical, winged monsters

intriguing
very interesting; fascinating

indicated
served as a sign of something; showed

Dragons Are:

➤ legendary reptiles

➤ symbols of destruction, evil, death, and sin in some cultures

➤ credited with having powers necessary to understand the secrets of the Earth in other cultures

➤ regarded by Chinese people as a symbol of good fortune

©Northwinds Picture Archive

Think About It

1. What makes maps in today's world more exact than maps in the past?

2. When ancient travelers wanted to know the distance between places, what did they do?

3. Ancient travelers judged the distance between places by how much time it took to go from one place to another. What types of transportation could you use in today's world to measure travel times?

4. Why do you think travelers exaggerated about what they had seen rather than providing exact descriptions?

5. Columbus thought he had sailed to Asia when he had actually sailed only to an island. What do you think Columbus would do if he knew that he had not reached Asia?

6. Why do you think people feared the unknown? When have you been fearful in an unfamiliar situation?

ATLAS:
A
BOOK
OF
MAPS

Where do we look for maps? We look in an atlas, of course. Have you ever wondered why a book of maps is called an atlas? What is the origin of the word *atlas*? And how is it related to maps? This is the story

5 of an ancient Greek named Atlas. By the time you come to the end, you'll understand why Atlas' name is **associated** with maps.

associated
related, connected

THE STORY OF ATLAS:
A GREEK MYTH

by Judy Rosenbaum

You have seen an atlas. It's a book of maps. But
the word *atlas* also has a different meaning. It was
10 someone's name. Here's the story of the first Atlas.

The ancient Greeks told tales about giant beings
called Titans. One Titan was named Atlas. The Titans
once fought against the Greek gods and lost. The gods
punished the Titans. Atlas' punishment was to hold
15 the sky up on his shoulders. He balanced the sky on his
shoulders for years and years and years.

Once Atlas almost got free. A hero named Hercules
came to see him. Hercules needed to locate some golden
apples. Only Atlas knew where they grew. Atlas said, "I'll
20 fetch the apples if you hold the sky up while I'm gone."

Hercules was almost as strong as a Titan. He held
the sky up while Atlas went for the apples. But it was
hard work. Soon, Atlas returned. He saw Hercules
with the sky on his shoulders. The weight of the sky
25 made Hercules sweat and groan. Who would want to
take back a job like that? Atlas thought, "I could leave
Hercules here and walk away. Then I would be free
forever."

Hercules **realized** what Atlas was thinking.
30 So Hercules thought of a trick. "This sky is very
uncomfortable!" he said. "Hold it up for a minute
while I put a pad on my shoulders. Then I'll hold it up
again." Unaware of the trick, Atlas took the sky from
Hercules.

realized
came to under-
stand; sensed

uncomfortable
feeling discomfort

35　　But the minute Hercules was free, he ran away. Atlas had to keep holding up the sky forever. In time, he turned into stone mountains—the Atlas Mountains in northwestern Africa. Even now, Atlas still seems to carry the sky on his shoulders.

40　　About 500 years ago, a great cartographer named Gerardus Mercator created a book of maps. In the book, he told the story of Atlas. Ever since then, a book of maps has been called an atlas.

Think About It

1. What do we call a book of maps?

2. Who were the Titans?

3. How did Hercules trick Atlas?

4. How do you think Atlas felt when Hercules outsmarted him?

5. What might have happened if Atlas didn't fall for Hercules' trick?

6. Have you ever had a particularly unpleasant job or chore? What are some of the ways of coping with an unfavorable task?

Floki: Sailor Without a Map

In days of old, a young man named Floki lived in **Norway**. He wanted to sail. He dreamed of faraway places. He heard of one beautiful place called **Iceland**. He dreamed of sailing to Iceland, but there were no
5 maps. He had no ship. Even if he got a ship, how would he get there? No map existed.

Years passed. At last, Floki had a ship and a crew. He was ready to sail. But Iceland was far away. He was told it was in the West. Floki set sail and headed west.
10 They sailed in an open boat. The ocean was **vast** and gray. The water was cold and the seas were rough. But there was something worse. Floki still had no map. He wondered how he would find Iceland without a map.

Floki had a plan. Floki took ravens on his ship. He
15 kept them caged. He waited. After they had been at sea for many days, he freed one bird. The first bird did not come back. It flew back the way they had come. What did that mean? Birds fly to the nearest land. The nearest

Norway
a country of Northern Europe

Iceland
an island nation in the North Atlantic

vast
very large, immense

The Norsemen and their raven pilot.

land was the land they had left. That
20 wasn't the way to Iceland. Floki kept
trying. He sent more ravens out. For
many weeks, they flew back to the
ship. No land was near.

Many months went by. The men
25 were hungry and cold. Floki worried
about them. He had to find Iceland!
One dark day, Floki freed two birds.
They flew ahead. They did not come
back. Their direction was clear.
30 They flew to the nearest land. Floki
followed them. He sailed after the
birds. He stayed the course. A few
days later, he could see land. His
dream had come true! He had
35 found it! He had found Iceland!

Think About It

1. Who was Floki? Where did he live?

2. What was Floki's dream? Why was his dream such a challenge?

3. What did Floki take with him on his trip? Why?

4. For weeks, ravens were freed but returned to the ship. No land was near. How do you think Floki and his men felt about how far they were from land?

5. If you were a sailor on Floki's ship, would you sign on for another journey with him? Why or why not?

6. Floki's dream came true. What is your greatest dream? What is the greatest challenge to making it come true?

Dig It!

STEP 1

Phonemic Awareness and Phonics

Unit 3 has three consonant sounds and one vowel sound. Letters represent the sounds.

- **Consonants:**

    g (gab, dig)

    d (dip, bad)

    v (vat)

Go to the **Consonant Chart** on page 209. Find the sounds for these letters: **g**, **d**, and **v**.

- **Vowel:** The vowel is short / *i* / spelled **i** (it, dim).

Go to the **Vowel Chart** on page 210. Find ĭ for short / *i* / on the chart. Find the example word: **sit**.

Word Recognition and Spelling

We put vowels and consonants together to make words. Every English word has at least one vowel. The examples use Unit 3 sound-spelling correspondences.

> **Examples: Unit Words**
>
> **in, dig, clip, list, live**

Some words are made up of two or more smaller words. These are called **compound words**. In a compound word, both words have to be real words that can stand on their own.

> **Example: Compound Word**
>
> **sand + bag = sandbag**

These are Unit 3 compound words.

> catnip   handbag
> granddad   sandbag
> grandstand   sandblast

Some words are made up of parts we call syllables. Sometimes one of the syllables can be used as a word but not the other. Sometimes neither syllable can be used by itself as a word. Together the parts make a **two-syllable word.**

> **Example: Two-Syllable Word**
>
> **ban + dit = bandit**

Note the pattern of vowels and consonants.

> **Example: VC/CV Pattern**
>
> **ban + dit = bandit**
> vc   cv = vc/cv

These are Unit 3 two-syllable words. They have the VC/CV pattern.

VC/CV

admit	fabric	plastic	transmit
attic	frantic	rabbit	victim
bandit	impact	tactic	
candid	mishap	traffic	
drastic	picnic	transit	

Essential Words

from, of, they, was, were, what

This is strange about the letter **v**: No English words end in **v**. At the end of a word, **v** is followed by **e**.

Examples: Words With **v**

have, give, live

Spelling Lists: The Unit 3 spelling lists contain two word categories:

1. Words with the three new consonants **g**, **d**, and **v** and short / i / spelled **i**

2. **Essential Words** (in italics)

Spelling Lists

Lessons 1–5		Lessons 6–10	
did	*they*	add	handbag
dig	van	clip	have
from	*was*	damp	list
gas	*were*	film	picnic
of	*what*	give	rabbit

3

Vocabulary and Morphology

Unit Vocabulary: Sound-spelling correspondences from this unit and previous units make up this unit's vocabulary.

- What do these words mean?
- Do some of them mean more than one thing? Which ones?

UNIT Vocabulary

g, d, v, i for short / *i* /

add	dim	had	lip	sand
and	draft	hand	list	sin
bad	drag	have	live	sip
bag	fig	hid	mad	sit
band	film	him	mint	slim
bib	fit	his	mitt	stand
big	flag	hit	picnic	tag
bit	gas	if	pig	tin
clip	gift	in	pin	traffic
crisp	give	inn	pit	transit
dad	glad	intrinsic	print	transmit
dam	grab	is	rabbit	trip
damp	grant	it	rib	
did	grin	land	rip	
dig	grip	lift	sad	

Word Relationships:

Words that have opposite meanings are **antonyms**. Think of opposites for the **Unit Vocabulary** words.

Words that have the same or similar meaning are **synonyms:** big/large; slim/thin; mad/angry. Think of synonyms for the **Unit Vocabulary** words.

Compound Words: Often the last part of a compound word names the item.

- A **sand<u>bag</u>** is a type of **bag**.
- A **grand<u>stand</u>** is a type of **stand**.

Meaning Parts

Review:

- Adding certain letters or punctuation to words can add to or change their meanings.
- Adding **-s** changes the word to mean more than one.

> **Example: Plural**
> gift**s**

- Adding **'s** signals possession or ownership.

> **Examples: Singular Possession**
> Tim**'s**, the pig**'s**

Grammar and Usage

Nouns may be common or proper:

- A **common noun** names a general person, place, or thing.
- A **proper noun** names a specific person, place, or thing.

> **Examples: Common and Proper Nouns**
>
> | Common Nouns | Proper Nouns |
> | --- | --- |
> | man | Mr. West |
> | city | Boston |
> | statue | Statue of Liberty |
> | land | Badlands |
> | mountains | Rockies |

Find common nouns on the **Unit Vocabulary** list.

Nouns may be concrete or abstract:

- A **concrete noun** names a person, place, or thing that we can see or touch.

> **Examples: Concrete Nouns**
> table, car, pencil, plate, teacher

- An **abstract noun** names an *idea* or a thought that we cannot see or touch.

> **Examples: Abstract Nouns**
> love, Saturday, sports, democracy

Nouns have several functions (or jobs).

- **Review:** A noun can be the **subject** of the sentence.
- A noun can be the **direct object**—the person, place, or thing that receives the action.

Read these Unit 3 nouns. They can be the subjects or direct objects in sentences.

Nouns

bag	flag	picnic	stand
band	gas	pig	tag
clip	gift	pin	traffic
dad	hand	pit	trip
dig	land	rabbit	valve
fig	lip	rib	van
film	mint	sand	

Some sentences have a **direct object**. The direct object is the person, place, or thing that receives the action. The predicate part of the sentence contains the verb and can include a direct object.

Use the sentence: Casey hit the ball.
            Subject   Predicate

- The subject answers: "Who did it?" **Casey**

- The predicate verb answers: "What did he do?" **hit**

- The direct object in the predicate answers: "Hit what?" **the ball**

The diagram below shows how to build this sentence with a subject, predicate, and direct object. Note the new sentence pattern: S/P/DO.

Form: N/V/N noun/verb/noun

Function: S/P/DO subject/predicate/direct object

Casey hit the ball. (*subject / predicate; action verb / direct object; noun*)

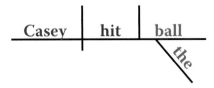

Listening and Reading

We read different types of text.

- Some text provides information. In informational text, we listen for and read the topic and details that support that topic. Details include ideas and facts.

- Some text tells a story. When we read a story, we listen or look for the parts of a story: characters, setting, events, and resolution.

Knowing the kind of text helps us focus on the right kind of information. When we focus on the right kind of information, we understand the text.

Why? Word History

Dig—*Dig* probably came into the English language from French in the 1300s. It may be related to the word *ditch*. What do *dig* and *ditch* have in common? Today, people often say they dig something they really like. *Dig* once meant "to study deeply"; if you dug something, you understood it well.

6

Speaking and Writing

We use different types of sentences when we speak and write.

Some sentences present facts. These are called statements.

> **Examples: Statements**
>
> **The map is flat.** This tells us a fact about the map.
>   What? It is flat.
>
> **The rabbit hid.** This tells us a fact about what the rabbit did.
>   What? It hid.

Some sentences ask for information. These are called questions. Many questions beginning with **what** require answers that *name a thing* or *identify the action*.

> **Examples: Questions**
>
> **What** is in the cab? The map is in the cab. *Map* tells **what** is in the cab.
>
> **What** did the man do? The man ran fast.
>   *Ran fast* tells **what** the man did.

More About Words

Expand vocabulary by learning these Bonus Words. Bonus Words use the same sound-spelling correspondences that we have studied in this unit and previous units.

UNIT Bonus Words

ad	fabric	grim	pad	snit
admit	fad	grit	pip	spin
attic	fib	handbag	plastic	sprint
bandit	fin	hint	prim	stilt
bid	fist	hip	primp	strand
bin	flint	imp	rag	strict
bland	flip	impact	rid	strip
blip	flit	jag	rift	tactic
brag	frantic	jilt	rig	tidbit
brand	gab	lag	rim	tilt
brim	gap	lid	sag	tint
candid	gland	limp	sandbag	tip
catnip	glib	lint	sandblast	trig
classic	glint	lisp	script	trim
crib	graft	lit	sift	valve
din	gram	mantis	silt	van
dip	grand	misfit	slid	vast
drab	granddad	mishap	slip	vat
drastic	grandstand	mist	slit	victim
drift	grasp	nag	snag	
drip	grid	nip	snip	

Stage Setting

An old saying says, "Don't count your chickens before they're hatched." As you read this cartoon, think of ways it might apply to these people.

Critic's Corner

1. What is a *draft*? Make a list of work that must be finished before a film can be produced.

2. What are these two planning? Are their plans realistic?

Stage Setting

We often misunderstand what is said. Sometimes, it's because we're thinking of a different meaning for a word.

Critic's Corner

1. What did each bat think? What caused their misunderstanding?

2. Misunderstanding can result in funny situations. Can it also cause bad situations? Give examples.

Stage Setting

Knowing your direction is important. Sometimes, maps are critical. Decide whether these people have planned well enough for their trip.

Critic's Corner

1. These flyers didn't have a map and they got lost. Have you ever been lost? Remember the situation.

2. Have you ever felt lost? Remember that situation. What is the difference between *being* lost and *feeling* lost?

Stage Setting

Sometimes, we are called on to do heroic deeds that we don't think we could do.

Critic's Corner

1. Beavers are known as hard workers. What do you know about these animals?

2. Do you think that an animal, like a beaver, could intentionally do a heroic deed? Or do you think that all animals in a species are exactly the same?

Stage Setting

Two ladies are shopping. They're looking at purses in the window of a boutique. Watch for the *pun* that follows.

Critic's Corner

1. A *pun* is a humorous use of a word or phrase to suggest more than one meaning. What is the pun in this cartoon?

2. Why do you think people often groan when they hear a pun?

Stage Setting

Sometimes, the unknown frightens us. Watch what happens when two people face the unknown in a dark, unfamiliar attic.

Critic's Corner

1. What is the most frightening thing these two could actually encounter in the grandmother's attic?

2. Think of a time you have been in an unfamiliar place, facing an unknown situation. Why are we less sure of ourselves in unfamiliar situations?

Stage Setting

Let's think about what *perspective* means. It means a point of view. Things look different from different points of view. Sometimes, it's good to see how others view things.

Critic's Corner

1. What do you suspect the ants think of the Big Dig?

2. Should the ants compare their digging skill with the machines used for the dig in Boston?

Stage Setting

Depending on where you live, different words have different meanings for you. These people are from Boston, Massachusetts.

Critic's Corner

1. Does the fact that these two men are from Boston give you a clue as to what they mean by the Big Dig? (You will read about the Big Dig later in this unit.)

2. What are their perspectives on the ants' Big Dig?

Stage Setting

Museums contain art masterpieces and science treasures. During the day, people visit, but at night strange things happen.

> What **are** they? Who **are** they? Can they stand?

> They can stand. They **grand**stand. Are they big, plastic plants?

> Are they big, abstract rabbits?

> They are big, misfit dinosaurs!

> Hmmm. They **are** trim.

Critic's Corner

1. The statues represent art; the dinosaurs represent science. Throughout history, people have argued about which is more important: science or art. Why?

2. Which do you think is more important? Give three specific reasons.

Stage Setting

One way that people play with words is a type of joke, called a *pun*. A pun is a humorous use of a word or phrase, suggesting more than one meaning. Watch for the pun here.

Critic's Corner

1. What is the pun in this cartoon? Why would it make some people groan?

2. Puns can be clever, but they're sometimes called *corny*. Why would we call something corny when it has absolutely nothing to do with corn? Go to the library at school and ask the librarian to help you find the answer.

Stage Setting

Every day, unexpected events slow us down. Let's watch our friendly aliens, and see what their *perspective* is. How do they view this situation?

Critic's Corner

1. Imagine the perspective of outside observers who know nothing about our transportation system. What are the aliens thinking?

2. What does *road rage* mean? Why do people become so angry about things they cannot control?

Stage Setting

Could dead dinosaurs have a perspective of their own? Watch what happens at our favorite dig site, and decide for yourself.

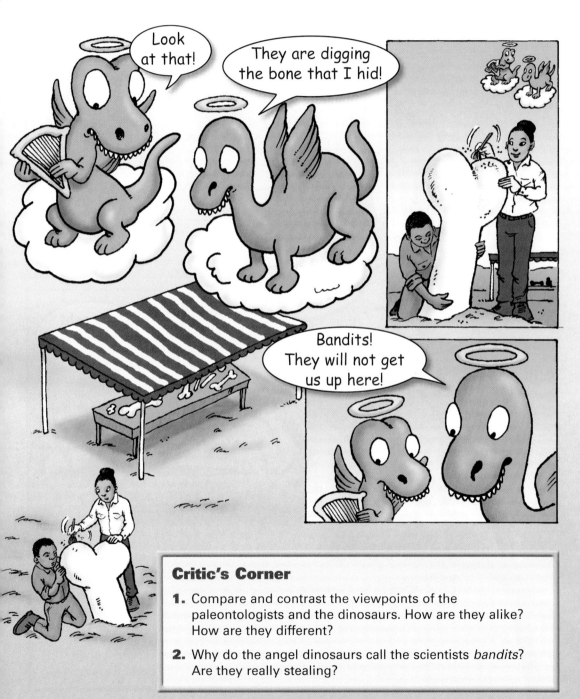

Critic's Corner

1. Compare and contrast the viewpoints of the paleontologists and the dinosaurs. How are they alike? How are they different?

2. Why do the angel dinosaurs call the scientists *bandits*? Are they really stealing?

Stage Setting

Some aliens are trying to figure out earthlings. Their perspective is based on the first things they see.

Critic's Corner

1. What conclusions have the aliens reached about earthlings? How were their perspectives formed?

2. Are our own perspectives formed based on things we see? Could these perspectives turn into prejudice?

Stage Setting

Many of us like participating in sports. Some who participate make excuses when they do not do well. Decide what you think about the participants in this wacky track meet.

Critic's Corner

1. The asp came in last in the track meet. What do you think her mishap might have been?

2. What did the pig complain about? Was the condition of the track worse for her than for the rabbit or the asp?

Stage Setting

Some people spend years, and continue working, because their goals are important. As you read this cartoon, think about these paleontologists' goals.

Critic's Corner

1. These two scientists are clearly disappointed. What might they have been looking for?

2. Think of a time when you have wanted something, have expected it, and yet have been disappointed.

Stage Setting

We often look at successful people and think of their lives as always busy. These two paleontologists can teach us something.

What is in your lab bag? Is it a fossil from your last dig?

From the last dig? No! This lab bag has figs and ham! Let's have a picnic!

I am famished!

Did you grab a plastic glass for me?

I have it. Can you find a picnic spot with no ants?

That's what they think.

Let's eat!

Critic's Corner

1. Do you think it is a good idea for these paleontologists to take a break from their work? Why?

2. What do you like to do when you take a break?

Africa Digs

In 1997, Dr. Paul Sereno led a dig. He took 18 scientists with him. They went to Africa. They went to **Niger**. The Touareg (*twä'rĕg*) tribe helped. The Touareg live in Niger. They know their land. They know it best. They
5 made the dig possible.

The dig was a success. They had a fantastic find. They found a new dinosaur. The Touareg have a legend. It tells of a very big animal. They call it *Jobar*. The scientists named the dinosaur. They called it
10 *Jobaria*. It means giant. Let's follow the dig. It has many steps.

Step 1: We've Got One!

The Touareg lead. The team follows. They spot a special place. Bones stick out of **desert** rock. The Touareg tell a story.
15 It is from the legend. These bones belong to the giant beast, *Jobar*.

Step 2: Digging In

The dig begins. They use tools. They use hammers and chisels. They use drills. They work for 10 weeks. A huge skeleton
20 **emerges**. It has been buried for 135 million years! Tons of rock cover it. The team takes the bones from the rock.

Step 3: Wrap It Up

They have to make "jackets." The jackets will protect the **fossils**. They use

Niger
a country of west-central Africa

desert
a dry region with little rainfall

emerges
comes out of; appears

fossils
remains of ancient creatures embedded in the earth's crust

The Touareg tribe helped the team.

25 paper. They use foil. They cut burlap strips. They dip
them in plaster. They wrap each bone. First, they cover
one side. The strip dries. Then, they cover the other
side. They number the jackets. They **log** each one. Dr.
Sereno keeps the dig's **log** book.

> **log**
> 1. to record in writing
> 2. a data record

Step 4: Move It Out

30 The team must go back to the lab. It is in Chicago.
Many tons of bones have to be moved. Some weigh
over 500 pounds. They have no machines. They use
a tripod. They use pulleys. They use rope. They use
chain. They load their trucks. They drive the bones to
35 the port. It is 1,000 miles away. They put the bones on
a ship. The ship crosses the Atlantic. Then, the bones
are sent to Chicago.

Step 5: Unwrap It

The team opens each piece.
They clean each bone. They
40 find the dig's log book. It has
the dig's records. Each jacket
has a number. They match the
numbers. Now, they begin. It's
time to rebuild the skeleton.

Step 6: Clean 'Em Up

45 This step takes two years.
They use dental tools. They
use tiny jackhammers. They
use chemicals. The work is
careful. It is precise. They have
50 to clean more than 200 bones.
These bones came from the
adult *Jobaria*. But they dug
up some other bones. These
were from young *Jobaria*.
55 They clean these, too.

*Dr. Paul Sereno and his team
at the African dig site.*

Dr. Paul Sereno examines the dinosaur bones.

Step 7: And the Missing Pieces?

Good luck! They have most of the adult's bones. What about the ones that are missing? They can make them. They use foam. They use clay.

Step 8: Make a Plan

All of the bones are clean. The missing bones are
60 made. At last, they make a model. From it, they create a blueprint. This is the plan to build the skeleton. First, they lay out the tail bones. They place them in order. Next, they study how to put them back together. They connect the bones. Now, the huge size of the dinosaur
65 is real.

Step 9: Copy the Fossils

fragile

easily damaged; delicate

Jobaria's bones are too heavy. They are very **fragile**. They cannot put them up. But they want to display them. What can they do? They copy the skeleton. They make molds. They create copies.

Step 10: Stack It Up

70   They attach the casts of the bones to a frame. The frame is made of steel. The hard steel frame is covered.

Finally: Share the Discovery!

They paint the casts. Now, the casts look like the real fossils. They are white. But they have bits of green and red. These 75 colors come from copper and iron in the soil. At last, they pose the dinosaur. It looks so real! You can almost hear that dinosaur roar!

Adapted from "Finding the Pieces...
and Putting Them Back Together Again"
by Michelle Laliberte

Answer It
Say the answer in a complete sentence.

1. Who led the dig in Niger, Africa?

2. Who lives in Niger?

3. Who helped Dr. Sereno with the dig?

4. What did the dig team find?

5. What is a legend?

6. What did the dig team make to protect the fossils?

7. What did they use to move 20 tons of bones?

8. What did they use to clean the bones?

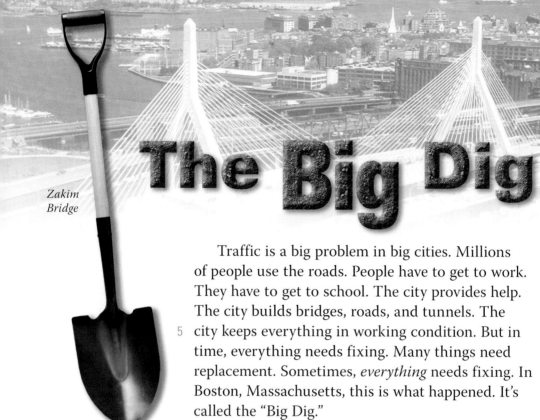

Zakim Bridge

The Big Dig

Traffic is a big problem in big cities. Millions of people use the roads. People have to get to work. They have to get to school. The city provides help. The city builds bridges, roads, and tunnels. The
5 city keeps everything in working condition. But in time, everything needs fixing. Many things need replacement. Sometimes, *everything* needs fixing. In Boston, Massachusetts, this is what happened. It's called the "Big Dig."

10   Boston had difficulties. It had terrible traffic jams. It had a particularly high accident rate. It had noise and air pollution. It had a lot of miserable drivers. Boston began the biggest **overhaul** ever attempted. They knew it would take years to finish. This is what they had to do:

overhaul

a large repair job; renovation

Overhaul Boston's Central Artery— the heart of its highway system.

15 1. Build a new bridge and tunnel system.
    2. Build them in the same spots where the original ones are now.
    3. Don't close any roads during construction.
    4. Build under water. Build through water. Build in
20   unstable **landfill** conditions.
    5. Dodge **foundations** of fragile historic buildings.
    6. Dodge skyscrapers.
    7. Don't tie up traffic.
    8. Don't make too much dust or noise. Don't disturb
25   the people of Boston.

landfill

a site where dirt has filled in low-lying ground

foundations

supportive bases on which buildings stand

Impossible? Not to the **civil engineers** who managed the Big Dig. Since 1959, everybody who drove into or out of Boston had to drive through the Central Artery. A million people had to use one part of 30 Interstate 93. There was no other way to go.

What could the city do?

Fred Salvucci was born in Boston. He was a civil engineer. He wanted to help his city. Fred suggested sinking the entire highway system. He suggested sinking it underground. He said it had to be wider. 35 Underground was the only place to go. Boston had become a huge city. If they tried to widen the current roads, they would run into buildings.

How did they do it?

Engineers met in the early 1980s. They began to design. They planned the biggest, most **complex** road 40 project in American history. Ten years later, in 1991, construction began. All over the world, the project became famous. It became known as the Big Dig.

complex

complicated, intricate

circumnavigate

to go all the way around; circle

The Big Dig Facts

- The Big Dig used lots of concrete. How much? Enough to build a 3-foot-wide sidewalk from Boston to San Francisco and back three times.

- More than 5,000 men and women worked on the Big Dig every day.

- The Big Dig used lots of steel. How much? Enough to make a 1-inch-thick steel bar. How long would the steel bar be? The bar could **circumnavigate** the Earth's equator.

Workers poured tons of concrete.

Southbay Interchange

I-93 North runs through a tunnel.

More than 12 years after that, Boston's new Central Artery/Tunnel
45 Project opened. It included three different types of tunnels. It has the largest cable bridge in the world. It has 161 lane-miles of new highway. These roads are in one 7.5-mile area. Boston has more
50 than 150 acres of new parks and open space.

Adapted from "Big Dig" by Laurie Ann Toupin

Think About It

1. Where did the Big Dig take place?

2. What was the purpose of the Big Dig?

3. Who was Fred Salvucci? What was Fred's profession? What important suggestion did Fred Salvucci make?

4. Pretend that you are Salvucci. Give reasons why putting the highway underground is a good idea.

5. Because of the Big Dig, the city of Boston has many new parks. What might be the benefits and the problems associated with these new parks?

6. Think of a problem facing your community. How would you solve it?

Dig This!

Shureice cleans dinosaur bones.

I was excited! I was going on a real dig! Would we find dinosaur bones? I was a normal 10th grader. For three weeks I got to be somebody special. I got to be a junior paleontologist. I got to hike in the Rockies. I got
5 to visit the Lewis and Clark Museum. I got to make discoveries on Egg Mountain. I even got to do some bird-watching. Best of all, I made new friends and had lots of fun.

Arriving

Here's what happened. Dr. Paul Sereno and his
10 wife, Gabrielle Lyon, have a special program called Project Exploration. I, Shureice Kornegay of Chicago, was selected to participate. We headed for Choteau, Montana. On the first day, along with my new friends, I headed for the Old Trail Museum. Here, we learned
15 our assignments. Paul Sereno and Gabrielle Lyon showed us around the museum. They told us we would be spending lots of time there.

Beginning

It was so exciting! I was a junior paleontologist on my first field trip! I didn't know what to expect. I had
20 never been to Montana. But I was up for the challenge. We began.

Montana dig site

Digging

We headed over to Pine Butte. This was an area of badlands. It was a large open space. It was hilly. Badlands are **barren** areas. They have rough, 25 **eroded** ridges, peaks, and **mesas**. Here, bones may be exposed. We split up into two groups. My group went prospecting. Our job: look around for bones. We climbed up a steep hill. We took out our pickaxes and dental tools. (Yes, dental tools.) We searched for a spot 30 to start. I couldn't wait to start digging! I knew we'd find those dino bones!

Discovering

We found a lot of calcite. Calcite is a bright, brittle rock. My friends and I thought that it looked just like bone. We learned a trick to know if the rocks were

barren
without plant life; unproductive

eroded
worn away

mesas
wide, flat-topped hills

35 actually bone. This was the "lick test." When you lick
a real bone, your tongue sticks to it because bone is
porous . Sound disgusting? Not really. Using the "lick
test," we found lots of small bones that we kept in sealed
plastic bags. I found the tip of a rib! We learned that
40 these bones are very fragile. We used a chemical that acts
like super glue. We used it to hold the rib tip together.

porous
having many small
holes or pores

Climbing

During the trip, we went on a 8-mile hike into the
Rockies. I got to lead the way for a bit. That was pretty
exciting! We filled up our water bottles at a freshwater
45 spring along the way. Our destination was over 7,000
feet up into the Rockies. We ended the day with a
barbecue at the museum. We learned about tribes that
had inhabited Montana hundreds of years ago. We told
some scary stories to see who we could spook. That
50 night, we roasted marshmallows.

We also got to visit Egg Mountain. Egg Mountain is
a place where many skeletons of the dinosaur *Maiasaura*
were found. Nests and babies were found there, too.
Maiasaura was about 30 feet long. Like many other
55 dinosaurs, it lived in the late Cretaceous Period. At this
site, we learned to recognize small fragments of eggshell.
These were dark, almost black, in the **sediment** . **Prolific**
bone beds, like the one at Egg Mountain, show that the
adult *Maiasaura* dinosaurs took care of their young.

sediment
a dirt-like substance
consisting of tiny
pieces of rock

Saying Good-bye

60 I was sad when our expedition ended. It was fun,
and I made many great friends.

prolific
having large
amounts; abundant

Adapted from "Fantastic Journeys:
Dig This!" by Shureice Kornegay

Think About It

1. Who is Shureice Kornegay? Where is her home? Where did she go on a trip?

2. How did Shureice describe the Badlands of Montana?

3. Why is calcite easily confused with bone? What is the name of the trick that the students used to distinguish between calcite and bone?

4. During the trip the students went on a hike into the Rocky Mountains. What might have been the positive and negative memories of this particular experience?

5. Shureice's trip allowed her to explore a subject that was interesting to her. If you could choose a subject to explore on a trip, where would you go? What would you explore?

6. Shureice kept a journal of her trip. You have just finished reading her journal. Have you ever kept a journal? Do you have a special time ahead of you, one that you'd like to remember?

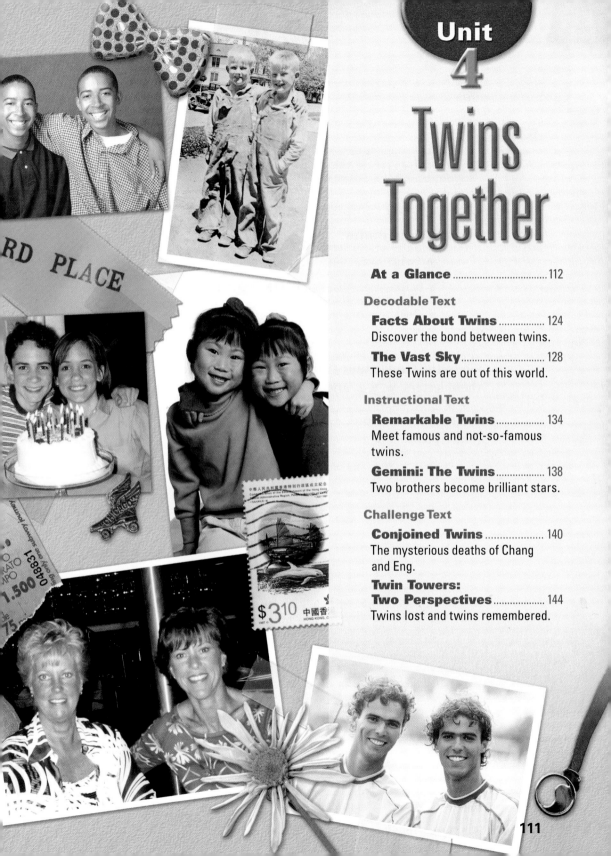

Unit
4
Twins
Together

STEP 1

Phonemic Awareness and Phonics

Unit 4 has four consonant sounds. Letters represent the sounds.

■ **Consonants:**

w (wig)

y (yap)

z (zip)

k (kid)

Go to the **Consonant Chart** on page 209. Find the sounds for these letters: **w**, **y**, **z**, and **k**.

At the end of a word, / k / is represented by the letters **-ck** (back, pick).

STEP 2

Word Recognition and Spelling

We put vowels and consonants together to make words. Every English word has at least one vowel. These examples use Unit 4 sound-spelling correspondences:

> **Examples: Unit Words**
>
> **win, yap, zip, kid, wick**

Some words are made up of two or more smaller words. These are called **compound words**. In a compound word, both words have to be real words that can stand alone.

> **Example: Compound Word**
>
> **back + track = backtrack**

Read these Unit 4 compound words.

backhand	pigskin
backpack	skinflint
backtrack	slapstick

Some words are made up of parts, called syllables. Sometimes one of the syllables is a word, but the other one is not. Sometimes neither syllable is a single word. A **two-syllable word** may also be a compound word.

A syllable that ends with a consonant sound is a **closed syllable**. A closed syllable contains a short vowel sound.

> **Examples: Closed Syllables**
>
> **map, hop, lit, bed**

Read these Unit 4 two-syllable words. They have the VC/CV pattern.

VC/CV

kidnap   napkin   zigzag

Essential Words

be, does, he, she, we, when

The sound / k / is spelled three ways. The position of / k / in the word signals how to spell it:

- Use **c** at the beginning of words before the vowel **a**: **c**at
- Use **k** at the beginning of words before the vowel **i**: **k**id
- Use **-ck** after one short vowel in one-syllable words: ba**ck**, si**ck**

Spelling Lists: The Unit 4 spelling lists contain two word categories:

1. Words with the four new consonants **w**, **y**, **z**, and **k** and the **-ck** spelling of / k /
2. **Essential Words** (in italics)

Spelling Lists

Lessons 1—5		Lessons 6—10	
ask	kick	backpack	sick
be	*she*	mask	skip
black	twin	milk	swim
does	*we*	napkin	wind
he	*when*	pack	zigzag

3 Vocabulary and Morphology

Unit Vocabulary: Sound-spelling correspondences from this unit and previous units make up this unit's vocabulary.

- What do these words mean?

- Do some of them mean more than one thing? Which ones?

UNIT Vocabulary

<u>w</u>, <u>y</u>, <u>z</u>, <u>k</u>, <u>-ck</u>

ask	kit	sick	swift	twist
back	lick	silk	swim	win
black	mask	skin	task	wind
brick	milk	skip	track	
jack	pack	snack	trick	
kick	pick	stack	twig	
kid	sack	stick	twin	

Idiomatic Expressions: An **idiomatic expression**, or idiom, is a common phrase that cannot be understood by the meanings of its separate words—only by the entire phrase. Its words cannot be changed, or the idiom loses its meaning.

Examples: Idiomatic Expressions

hit the sack = go to bed

do the trick = bring about the desired result

stick to your ribs = be substantial or filling (used with food)

Word Relationships Review:

- Words that have opposite meanings are **antonyms**.
  Think of opposites for the **Unit Vocabulary** words.
- Words that have the same or similar meaning are **synonyms**: big/large; swift/fast; mad/angry.
  Think of synonyms for the **Unit Vocabulary** words.

Compound Words: In some compound words, the last part of the word does not name the item. Sometimes the first part and the last part can combine together to form an entirely new meaning.

The meaning is not always the sum of the parts. The meaning is not always a *type* of the last word in the compound.

Both **big** and **wig** are words, but **bigwig** is not a type of **wig**.

Both **cat** and **nip** are words, but **catnip** is not a type of **nip**.

Meaning Parts: Adding certain letters or punctuation to words can add to or change their meanings. Adding **-s** to a word can mean two different things:

Review:

- Adding **-s** adds meaning to a word. It means more than one (gifts).
- Adding **-s** also signals the person and tense (time) of the verb: **-s** means third person singular present tense. (See Step 4: Grammar and Usage.)

> **Examples: Third Person Singular Present Tense**
> he **sits**, she **raps**, it **kicks**.

STEP

4 Grammar and Usage

Pronouns are function words that are used in place of nouns. Different groups of pronouns have different functions.

Nominative (subject) **pronouns** (**I, you, he, she, it, we, you, they**) take the place of the subject in a sentence.

> **Example: Nominative Pronoun**
> Jack sat in a cab. **He** sat in a cab.
> (**He** replaces Jack in the sentence.)

A **phrase** is a group of words that does the same job as a single word.

A **preposition** is an English function word that begins a prepositional phrase. A **prepositional phrase** begins with a preposition and ends with a noun or pronoun that is the object of the preposition. The preposition shows the position or relationship to the noun or pronoun. Some prepositions include: **at, in, from**.

> **Example: Prepositional Phrase**
>
> **in the cab**
>
> **in** *(preposition)* the **cab** *(object of the preposition)*
> "in" shows the relationship to "the cab"

Verbs describe action. Verbs also show time. If something is happening today, it is the **present tense**.

Tense Timeline

Yesterday	Today	Tomorrow
Past	Present	Future
	-s	

Verb endings signal the time. Specific endings signal present tense: **-s** as in sit**s**, rap**s**, kick**s**.

At a Glance 117

Read these Unit 4 verbs. Say them again and add **-s**.

Verbs			
ask	pick	skip	win
crack	risk	swim	yak
kick	sack	track	zap
pack	skid	twist	zip

Adverbs are an English word class.

- One job of adverbs is to describe verbs.

- Adverbs can be single words (daily, suddenly).

- Some prepositional phrases act like adverbs.
  They begin with a preposition and end with a noun
  (on Monday, in the house, with a bang, to the class).

- Adverbs and prepositional phrases that act as adverbs tell
  when, **where**, and **how**.

The **predicate** part of the sentence contains the verb and can
include:

- A **direct object**.

- An **adverb** or **prepositional phrase that acts as an adverb**
  and tells **when**, **where**, or **how**.

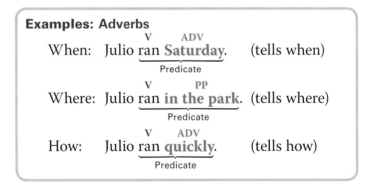

Examples: Adverbs

$$\underset{\text{Predicate}}{\underbrace{\overset{\text{V}}{\text{ran}}\ \overset{\text{ADV}}{\textbf{Saturday}}}}$$

When: Julio ran **Saturday**. (tells when)

Where: Julio ran **in the park**. (tells where)

How: Julio ran **quickly**. (tells how)

Adverbs, prepositional phrases that act as adverbs, and direct
objects expand the predicate of the sentence.

The diagram below shows how to build a sentence with a subject, predicate, and adverb.

Form: **N/V/ADV**   **noun/verb/adverb**
Function: **S/P/ADV**   **subject/predicate/adverb**

The class worked carefully.

subject; noun / predicate; action verb / adverb

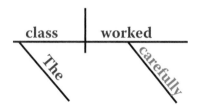

5 Listening and Reading

We read different kinds of text.

- Some text provides information. In informational text, we listen and read for the topic and details that support that topic. Details include ideas and facts.

- Some text tells a story. When we read a story, we listen or look for the parts of a story: characters, setting, events, and resolution.

Knowing the type of text helps us focus on the information. When we focus on the right kind of information, we understand the text.

STEP 6

Speaking and Writing

We use different types of sentences when we speak and write.

Some sentences present facts and opinions. These are called statements.

> **Examples: Statements**
>
> **The twins are remarkable.** This tells us an opinion about the twins. What? They are remarkable.
>
> **The man worked at the Big Dig.** This tells us a fact about the man. What? He worked at the Big Dig.
>
> **They shipped the bones to Chicago.** This tells us a fact about the bones. What? They were shipped to Chicago.

Some sentences ask for information. These are called questions. Questions beginning with **when** require answers that give a time.

> **Examples: Questions**
>
> **When** did he run? He ran yesterday.
> *Yesterday* tells **when** he ran.
>
> **When** did it snow? It started to snow before school ended.
> *Before school ended* tells **when** it snowed.
>
> **When** is his birthday? His birthday is on July 4th.
> *July 4th* tells **when** his birthday is.

More About Words

Expand vocabulary by learning these Bonus Words. Bonus Words use the same sound-spelling correspondences that we have studied in this unit and previous units.

UNIT Bonus Words

backhand	disk	rack	slapstick	wisp
backpack	flick	risk	slick	wit
backtrack	frisk	skid	smack	yak
bask	kidnap	skim	tack	yam
blitz	kin	skim milk	tick	yap
brisk	lack	skimp	wag	zap
clack	napkin	skinflint	wick	zigzag
click	nick	skit	wig	zip
crack	pigskin	slack	wilt	

Idiom	Meaning
be in the swim	active in the general current of affairs
be in the wind	likely to occur; in the offing
be on the rack	be under great stress
do the trick	bring about the desired result
hit the sack	go to bed
kick the habit	free oneself from addiction, as cigarettes
pat on the back	congratulate; encourage someone
stick to your ribs	be substantial or filling (used with food)

Why? Word History

Twi—The words *twin*, *two*, *twenty*, *twilight*, *twice*, and *twig* all have something in common. They come from the Old English word *twi*, which meant the number "two." So, a twig divides a branch into two parts. Twilight divides a 24-hour period into two parts, day and night.

Facts About Twins

Have you ever met twins? Have you ever been surprised to learn that someone you knew had a twin? Meet some remarkable twins.

TEACHER: Today we are reading facts about some interesting twins.

Elvis and His Twin

TEACHER: The first set of twins is Elvis and Jesse Presley. They were born in 1935. Elvis Presley was a famous singer. His twin brother, Jesse, died at birth. When were they born?

STUDENT: **Elvis and his twin were born in 1935.**

TEACHER: Who was Jesse's famous twin?

STUDENT: **His twin was Elvis.**

TEACHER: Elvis sold more records than anyone. Recordings that sell more copies than others are called hits. Elvis had 18 number one songs. How popular was Elvis?

STUDENT: **Elvis had 18 #1 hits.**

TEACHER: Elvis is often called the "King of Rock and Roll." Teenage girls screamed when they watched him sing. An idiom for liking someone or something a lot is to "flip your lid." Paraphrase this sentence using this idiom: "Fans go crazy for Elvis."

STUDENT: **Fans "flip their lids" for him.**

TEACHER: Elvis also made many movies in which his singing was a prominent feature. What else did Elvis do besides make records?

STUDENT: Elvis was in hit films.

TEACHER: In Elvis' day, a slang word for a home was a "pad." Elvis' home as an adult was in Memphis. He named his home Graceland. Use slang to paraphrase.

STUDENT: His pad was Graceland.

TEACHER: Elvis was nominated for a Grammy 15 times.

STUDENT: What did Elvis win?

TEACHER: During his career, Elvis won three Grammies for his music.

TEACHER: When Elvis died, he was buried at his home in Memphis. He was buried beside his twin, Jesse. Where are these twins buried?

STUDENT: Elvis and his twin are at Graceland.

TEACHER: Since his death, thousands of people visit Graceland every year to honor "the King." What can you say about Elvis?

STUDENT: Elvis is famous. Ask a fan if he lives!

The Baker Twins

TEACHER: The first set of twins we read about were males. The next set of twins is female. Their names are Kari and Kim Baker. Who is Kari?

STUDENT: **She is Kim's twin.**

TEACHER: Where do the twins live?

STUDENT: **Kari and Kim Baker live in a small town in a northern state called Montana.**

TEACHER: Kari and Kim have a ranch in Montana. They raise horses. They have lots of dogs and cats and even a pet pig. Tell me about some of their animals.

STUDENT: **They have a pack of pets. The twins have cats, horses, and a pig!**

TEACHER: These two twins are inseparable. That means they can't imagine being apart. They have always lived together. Paraphrase how the twins seem to be.

STUDENT: **The twins are connected.**

TEACHER: They stay in shape with their work at the ranch. How do the twins stay in shape? I'll say the sentence using "Kari," then you say it using "Kim": "Kari has tasks."

STUDENT: **Kim has tasks.**

TEACHER: Paraphrase: "The twins are in shape."

STUDENT: **The twins are fit.**

TEACHER: I'd like you to paraphrase again: "Kim and Kari are best friends."

STUDENT: **The twins admit they are pals.**

TEACHER: When the horses' hooves or manes need to be trimmed, Kari and Kim work together. What chore do the twins do together?

STUDENT: **The twins trim the horses.**

TEACHER: Since they live up north, they have to cut firewood. Another word for "cut" is "split." Paraphrase this sentence: "Both Kari and Kim cut firewood."

STUDENT: **The twins split wood.**

TEACHER: Kari and Kim live up north. They use the firewood to keep warm. Other words that mean "cold" are "crisp" and "brisk." Use these words to describe how the air feels when you need a fire.

STUDENT: **It is crisp and brisk.**

TEACHER: The sisters disagree on one thing. Kari says their horses can't tell them apart. Kim says they can. Did Kim say the horses can or cannot tell which twin is which?

STUDENT: **Kim said they can.**

TEACHER: Let's summarize. While these twins are not famous on a grand scale, they are famous in Libby, Montana! They have their animals to make their lives feel complete. Most importantly, they have each other. Say these sentences using the other twin's name: "Kari's twin is a big fan of Kari." "Kari is a big fan of her twin."

STUDENT: **Kim's twin is a big fan of Kim. Kim is a big fan of her twin.**

TEACHER: We've read about some remarkable twins. We met a rock and roll star and Montana ranchers! What is this selection's title?

STUDENT: **It is "Facts About Twins."**

The Vast Sky

Twins come in all shapes and sizes. Sometimes they appear in the most unexpected places.

These twins are found in the sky.

TEACHER: These twins are celestial. Celestial means that they are found in the sky as opposed to on Earth. Where are these twins found?

STUDENT: **The twins are in the vast sky.**

TEACHER: The celestial twins are located in the constellation Gemini. What kind of stars does the constellation Gemini contain?

STUDENT: **It has twins.**

TEACHER: Constellations are manmade, artificial ways to recognize clusters of stars in the sky. Designs have been drawn around these groups of stars and given names. The lines don't exist. In other words, they are not real. We have to imagine the lines and create a picture of the real thing in our minds. We use the word "abstract" when we try to imagine real objects when they don't exist. We use the word "concrete" for objects that are real. Is a constellation concrete or abstract?

STUDENT: **It is abstract.**

TEACHER: What about a star?

STUDENT: Is it abstract?

TEACHER: No, a star is real. It is concrete, but the constellation is abstract. Let's talk about the designs that have been drawn around these star patterns and then given names. We've already learned that

This 17th century Persian illustration shows the constellation Gemini.

the twin stars are in Gemini. Everyone on Earth sees these constellations. When an Arab first saw this constellation, however, he called it something different.

STUDENT: **What did he name it?**

TEACHER: The Arab named it "twin peacocks." The Egyptians called the constellation the "twin plants." What was it called by the Egyptians?

STUDENT: **Its name was the twin plants.**

TEACHER: In the Hindu population, this same constellation was known by yet another name. What did they name it?

STUDENT: **The Hindus called it the "twin gods."**

TEACHER: There are many other named constellations. You have probably heard of some. The zodiac symbols are examples of some of these constellations. A set of imaginary lines has been drawn around the stars of Gemini. These lines come together to represent a pair of twins. Thus, Gemini is called the Twins. Paraphrase this sentence.

STUDENT: **It stands for the Twins.**

TEACHER: Each zodiac symbol represents a set time period on our calendar. Gemini is associated with late May and June. Aries is another zodiac symbol, which is associated with late March and April. The animal symbol for Aries is the Ram. Paraphrase this sentence.

STUDENT: **It stands for the Ram.**

TEACHER: Cancer the Crab is linked to the summer months of June and July. What does Cancer stand for?

STUDENT: **It stands for the Crab.**

TEACHER: People have been studying the stars for thousands of years. They began looking for ways to bring these faraway objects closer to us. When did people start wondering about the stars?

STUDENT: **It was in the past.**

TEACHER: Let's talk about how ancient people used the stars. One way they used the stars was to navigate or steer their ships. They used them to plan their trips. How did ancient sailors use the stars?

STUDENT: **They used them to plan trips.**

TEACHER: To help them navigate across the oceans, they made maps of the stars. I'll say a sentence in past tense. You change it to present tense: "The sailors mapped the stars."

STUDENT: **They map the stars.**

TEACHER: Farmers needed to know when to plant different crops during the year.

STUDENT: **When did they plant?**

TEACHER: Farmers planted their crops according to the stars. Certain arrangements of the constellations in the night sky told them it was time to plant. Sometimes, farmers planted seeds. Other times, they set out sprigs, or small plants. What can a man plant in his fields instead of seeds?

STUDENT: A man can plant sprigs.

TEACHER: Tell me two ways people used stars in the past.

STUDENT: They were used to plan trips and to plant sprigs.

TEACHER: People everywhere have used the abstract concept of constellations to help them break the sky into segments or bits. By dividing the sky into segments or constellations, people can more easily remember the location and name of the countless stars in the sky. Why did people create the concept of constellations?

STUDENT: **It splits the sky in segments.**

TEACHER: An astronomer's job is to search, or scan, the heavens for stars and planets. Tell me the first part of his job.

STUDENT: **His task is to scan the sky.**

TEACHER: He names his discoveries and shares them with other scientists. Tell me another part of an astronomer's job.

STUDENT: **His task is to name the stars.**

TEACHER: Stars seem to move across the sky. They really don't move, but the Earth does. It spins on its axis. The Earth is also at an angle, or tilt. The Earth's rotation makes the stars appear to move. What does the Earth do to make the constellations appear to move in the sky?

STUDENT: **It tilts and spins.**

TEACHER: Although the stars do not move, other objects in the sky do move. Satellites travel across the sky and are visible at night. When a satellite orbits in the night sky, it may be barely visible. How could we describe its brightness?

STUDENT: **In the vast sky, it is dim.**

TEACHER: Satellites are used to send information through space from one place on Earth to another. Use synonyms to replace "send" with "transmit" and "information" with "facts": A satellite is used to send information.

STUDENT: It is used to transmit facts.

TEACHER: It's time to review some of the facts from this selection. The constellation Gemini has bright twin stars. What is significant about the constellation Gemini?

STUDENT: It has twin stars.

TEACHER: Twelve constellations have been linked to our calendar. These are called the signs of the zodiac. We hit on three of the zodiac signs in this selection. What are they?

STUDENT: We hit on the Twins, the Ram, and the Crab.

TEACHER: Right. Gemini represents the Twins. Aries stands for the Ram. The Crab represents Cancer. While constellations appear to move across the sky, really the Earth's rotation causes this illusion. What does the Earth do to make the stars seem to drift?

STUDENT: It tilts and spins.

TEACHER: Finally, we talked about other things we see in the night sky, like satellites. We learned they help us communicate by sending information. What does a satellite do?

STUDENT: It transmits facts.

TEACHER: What is the title of this selection?

STUDENT: It is "The Vast Sky."

Remarkable Twins

These twins have done special things. Their lives are unusual. Read about them. Learn what it's like to be a twin.

Elvis Aron and Jesse Garon Presley

Elvis Aron Presley was born in 1935. Where? He
5 was born in Mississippi. He was King of Rock and Roll. Everyone knows about Elvis. But what about Jesse? Do you know about him? Jesse was Elvis' brother. He was his twin. Jesse died at birth.

It was Christmas 1946. Elvis wanted a bike. His
10 parents couldn't afford it. Instead, he got a guitar. It cost $12.95. That was just the beginning. Elvis made

history. He sold more records than anyone. He had 18 number one songs. He had 15 Grammy **nominations** . He won three.

15

Elvis was **remarkable** . At times, he spoke of his twin. He never knew his brother. Yet, he always felt connected to him. Elvis died in 1977. He was

20 in Memphis. He was at home. His home's name was Graceland. After that, Graceland opened its doors. Now, people can visit. Elvis and Jesse are buried there. They were

25 born together. In the end, they are together again.

nominations
recommendations for awards or honors

remarkable
notable, extraordinary

Kim and Kari Baker

2,500 people live in Libby. Where's Libby? It is in Montana. It has a drive-in. It has two **llama** farms. It has something else. It has Kim and

30 Kari Baker. The Bakers are ranchers. They are also photographers.

These twins were born in Montana. They lived there until their teens. Then, they moved to Florida. They loved horses. For years, they showed horses. They

35 have always loved the outdoors. They missed Montana. They went back in 1988. They became ranchers.

They have always been close. They have the same interests. They help each other. They take turns feeding the horses. They both cut firewood. (They need it for

40 their home.) They work together. Is it time to trim horses' hooves? Kari trims the right side. Kim trims the left.

Can their horses tell them apart? Kari says they can't. Kim thinks they can. ". . . the horses *can* tell us apart. Animals are more **aware** than people."

llama
a domesticated animal related to the camel

aware
watchful, conscious of

Scott Kelly

Mark Kelly

Mark and Scott Kelly

45   Mark and Scott Kelly are twins. They grew up in New Jersey. Both became **astronauts**. In 1996 they applied. 35 candidates were selected. 3,500 had applied. NASA selected both Kellys. What is the chance of *both* being selected? Can you figure it out? Ask your math teacher
50 for help!

    The Kellys became the first twins to fly in space. In 1999, Scott went up. He became the first twin in space. He flew a shuttle. He flew on *Discovery*. What did he do? He worked on the Space Telescope.

55   Two years later, it happened. Mark got a mission. He flew *Endeavour*.

    What else do the Kellys have in common? Both are space shuttle pilots. Both are test pilots. Both are **combat** pilots. Both are Navy lieutenant commanders. Both are
60 engineers. Both are married. Their daughters are the same age. They even play on the same soccer team!

    In 2003, *Columbia* met tragedy. The future is not sure. But the Kellys will return to space. They are sure of that.

> **astronauts**
> people trained for space flight

> **combat**
> relating to battle

Adapted from "Twin Portraits" and "Twinnacle of Success"
by Craig Sanders, Twinstuff.com

Answer It
Say the answer in a complete sentence.

1. When was Elvis born? When did Jesse die?

2. When did Elvis get a guitar?

3. When did Kim and Kari Baker live in Montana?

4. Where did the Baker twins begin to work with horses?

5. Does Kim like to be away from Kari?

6. When did NASA select both Kellys?

7. When did Scott become the first twin to fly?

8. What was Mark's first mission?

Gemini: The Twins

Castor Pollux

constellation

a group or pattern of stars

stars

heavenly bodies seen as points of light in the night sky

poets

writers of verse

Some night, look at the sky. Look for the **constellation** Gemini. It has two very bright **stars**. They are called the Twins. They have been known for thousands of years. They have always been in the sky.

5   Ancient people talked about them. The Greeks said they were the sons of Zeus and Leda. What did others call these two stars? Arabs called them twin peacocks. Egyptians called them twin plants. Hindus called them twin gods.

What are constellations?

10   What are constellations? First, they are not real. They are ideas. The stars exist. But the constellations do not. These were made up. **Poets** told stories about them. So did people everywhere. How long have we put stars in groups? We have done it for at least 6,000

15 years.

Why did the idea of constellations begin?

Why were star groups made up? There are so many stars! How could we remember them all? We could put them in groups! The groups break the sky into parts. They help us remember which stars are which. How
20 many can we see? On a dark night, we see 1,000 to 1,500 stars. Where can we see the Twins? We can see them in the north. When? We can see them in November through April. We can see them in the south, too. When? We can see them in December through March.

The ancient Greek story of Gemini

25 Zeus and Leda had twin sons. Their names were Castor and Pollux. They were devoted. They were loving brothers. They looked alike. But they were not alike. Castor was **mortal**. He became a horseman. Pollux was **immortal**. He became a boxer. Both
30 became expert soldiers. Castor was killed in battle. Pollux could not bear to be without his twin. Pollux asked his father, Zeus, for help. He asked for Castor to come back to life. Zeus agreed. They are side by side. They are stars forever. They are the Twins. They are
35 the two **brilliant** stars in Gemini.

mortal
destined to eventually die

immortal
not destined to die; eternal

brilliant
extremely bright, radiant

Answer It
Say the answer in a complete sentence.

1. What is Gemini?

2. Why were star groups made up?

3. When did the study of stars begin?

4. How many stars can be seen on a dark night?

5. When is Gemini seen in the north?

6. When is Gemini seen in the south?

7. When did Castor and Pollux become stars?

8. Who made Castor and Pollux into brilliant stars?

Conjoined Twins

Chang and Eng

Chang and Eng are famous. They were conjoined twins. They were born in Siam (now Thailand). They were joined at the chest. What connected them? A thick band of tissue. Doctors argued. Could they be
5 separated successfully?

Chang and Eng lived long lives. They lived to be 63. Both had married. Between them, they had 22 children. This is their story.

Eng and Chang Bunker died on a cold January
10 night in 1874. They left the world as they entered it 63 years before—together. Their lives had raised eyebrows. They had also raised questions. Would one twin's death cause the death of the other? This question was answered when they died.

15 Or was it?

The cause of Eng's death is not known. Chang had suffered a stroke four years before. His health had become **frail**. He was also a heavy drinker. He had recently been hurt in a **carriage** accident. He had
20 **bronchitis**. Eng, on the other hand, had been in good health. He was not affected by his brother's poor health.

After their deaths, doctors disagreed. Chang had died of a blood clot. Some doctors thought that Eng had died of shock. In other words, Eng was literally

frail
weak, sickly

carriage
an elegant wheeled vehicle pulled by a horse

bronchitis
an infection in the tubes leading to the lungs

*Chang and Eng Bunker
were born in Siam.*

25 scared to death. Others believed that the band that
connected the twins was a lifeline. They believed the
band passed death from one to the other. They found
the blood clot in Chang's brain. But it did not explain
Eng's death.

30   How had their lives begun? The boys learned to
run, jump, and swim. They had perfect coordination.
Exercise stretched their connection, from 4 inches to 5½.
They turned 8. Their father died. By age 14, the two were
selling duck eggs. They had to provide for the family.

merchant

a person who buys and sells things for a living

35 About this time, Chang and Eng were discovered. Robert Hunter, a British **merchant**, convinced their mother to let them go. He said that her boys had a great future. He said that they could become rich. It was three years before the king let them leave Siam.

40 Their mother had sold the boys to Hunter for $3,000. Happily, the agreement would end in 2½ years. The boys would be free at 21. Their mother only got $500.

Hunter and his partner managed the twins. They showed them in theaters and concert halls. They worked 45 in America and England. Admission was 50 cents. The managers pushed the twins. It was exhausting. They toured constantly. They had little rest.

Then the twins turned 21. They became independent. Chang and Eng had been Siamese boys 50 with no knowledge of the outside world. Now they had become worldly men. They were interested in learning and culture.

"Conjoined twins" is the correct term for twins who are physically joined. The term "Siamese twins" is derogatory.

Many newspaper articles described the twins. Chang was an inch shorter than his brother. But he 55 made up for it in temper. Chang was thought to be the dominant brother. He was mentally faster, but faster to anger. Eng was quieter. Eng had wider interests than Chang. These traits hardened in their later lives.

In spite of minor differences, the twins continued 60 to amaze people. Their relationship seemed good. With few exceptions, they acted as one. They shared tastes and opinions. Some thought that they were **telepathic**. After all, the two rarely spoke to one another!

telepathic

communication without using senses

The twins applied for and received U.S. citizenship. 65 It was then that they adopted their last name, Bunker. They proposed to two sisters, Adelaide and Sarah (Sally) Yates. Chang married Addie. Eng married Sally. At first, the girls' parents forbade the marriages. They gave in when they learned that the four planned to elope.

70 At that point, Chang and Eng wanted to risk a surgery. They would try separation. They went to Philadelphia. Surgeons were ready. Just before the knife was used, Sally

and Adelaide appeared. Their pleading and weeping sent their future husbands home—still joined.

75   In their last years, the twins argued. During one quarrel Chang threatened Eng with a knife. Furious, the two went to their family doctor. They demanded immediate separation. Calmly, the surgeon laid out his instruments. He turned to them and asked a question.

80   "Which would you **prefer**? Shall I sever the flesh that connects you? Or shall I cut off your heads? One will produce the same result as the other." This was enough to cool the twins' tempers.

    Their doctor made a promise. He would perform the
85 operation immediately upon the death of either one of the brothers. Sadly, he was not present when Chang died.

prefer
to choose or select a more desirable option

Think About It

1. Where were Chang and Eng joined?

2. At age 63, Chang died of a blood clot. What was the cause of Eng's death?

3. Chang and Eng were identical twins. They looked alike. In what ways were they different?

4. When Chang and Eng learned that the surgery to separate them might end their lives, they quickly reconsidered. Do you think their decision improved their relationship? Why or why not?

5. Some people mistreat people who are different. Why do you think they do this? If you could, what would you say to these people?

6. Suppose you were conjoined to a twin, and you could not be separated. How would life be more difficult for you? Think of at least six things that would be very difficult.

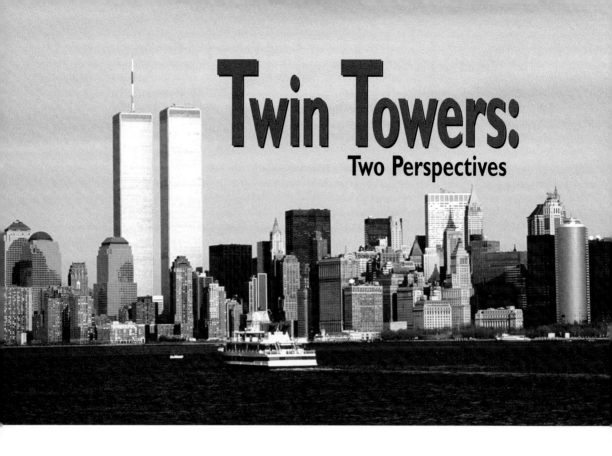

Twin Towers:
Two Perspectives

Eyewitness: The Twin Towers Fall

TUESDAY, 11 SEPTEMBER, 2001, 16:51 GMT 17:51 UK
PANIC-STRICKEN NEW YORKERS FLED THE
COLLAPSING WORLD TRADE CENTER.

BBC News Online's David Schepp was near the
5 *Twin Towers of the World Trade Center when they*
collapsed.

The felling of the Twin Trade Towers is a scene that
no New Yorker will ever forget.

Shortly after 0900 local time, thousands gathered
10 on the sidewalks of New York to view an improbable
scene. Two gaping, flaming holes in the side of both
towers caused by planes flown **deliberately** and
directly into them.

On the streets below, crowds gathered wherever
15 there was a view of the smoking towers. People's
reactions ranged from stunned disbelief to weeping.

deliberately

on purpose,
intentionally

Others pitched in, doing what they could to direct traffic or assist people.

Along 6th Avenue, New Yorkers stood **aghast** as
20 they watched the buildings burn, and a sudden shriek went up when the south tower collapsed, sending a huge plume [of] dust into the air.

People ran screaming as a growing cloud of **debris** hit the streets of lower Manhattan and pushed them up
25 the Avenue.

It was like the scene out of a movie as the huge ball of rubble grew behind a terrorized crowd running for cover.

Shortly after the first tower went down, the second collapsed, sending more smoke and debris into the air.
30 Further uptown, trolleys formed outside St. Vincent's Medical Centre in Greenwich Village awaiting the injured.

Hospital staff went through the crowd, pleading with people to donate blood.
35 Shopkeepers shut-up shop, while others remained open as employees gathered around televisions and radios to hear what had happened.

Major north-south **thoroughfares** were shut down for access to police and emergency vehicles only, as
40 pedestrians made their way uptown.

A Personal Reflection: A Twin Remembers the Twin Towers

DATE: SEPTEMBER 11, 2001. I was in a car with my twin brother. We were listening to the radio. A news report came on. We listened. We were stunned. A plane had struck one of the Twin Towers. We kept
45 listening. We heard live radio interviews. New Yorkers were horrified. We heard **vivid** details. We listened as the second Twin Tower was hit by another plane.

Days passed. We learned more about the victims. I found myself paying attention to victims who were
50 twins. I read interviews. One twin (a little girl) said it well. "I felt bad. I'm a twin. Just like the buildings were. I don't know what I would do. What if I lost my twin?"

aghast
shocked, horrified

debris
scattered wreckage, rubble

thoroughfares
main roads or streets

vivid
realistic, graphic

Clouds of dust and debris fill the air as the Twin Towers fall.

perished
died in an untimely or violent way

I began thinking. What did these buildings mean to me? Remembering the 55 towers, I realized something. Being a twin was central to my life. Most of my life involves my family. My family includes my twin. It includes my wife and her twin. Now, it includes our twin sons.

60 Every story was important. Every loss was significant. But I kept thinking of specific heroes. I thought about the twin firefighters. They were there when the buildings collapsed. One **perished**. 65 His twin survived. I think about young twins who lost their parents. I mourn for the twins who were left behind.

I think of the buildings themselves. They symbolized human achievement. 70 They will always be emotional symbols. The Twin Towers were built together. They fell together. Identical twins, from birth to death.

Adapted from "Twin Powers:
A Twin's Thoughts on the World Trade
Center's Twin Towers" by Craig Sanders, Twinstuff.com

Think About It

1. What was the date of the attack on the Twin Towers at the World Trade Center in New York City?

2. What were two ways that people helped after the towers were hit?

3. How did people eventually name the date and the event? Can you think of any other significant dates in United States history?

4. The twin who "remembers the Twin Towers" kept a journal about the attack. How is journal writing different from news reporting, as in the BBC report?

5. Being a twin was central to the author's life. What are some things that are central to or very important in your life? Why are these things important to you?

Jazz It Up

Phonemic Awareness and Phonics

Unit 5 has words that end in double letters and two vowel sounds.

■ **Double Consonants**

The sounds / s /, / f /, / l /, and / z / are usually represented by double letters **-ss**, **-ff**, **-ll**, and **-zz** (pass, miff, doll, jazz) at the end of words.

■ **Vowels:**

The letter **o** represents two different vowel sounds:

short / o /   (hop, lock)

/ aw /   (off, dog, toss)

Go to the **Vowel Chart** on page 210.

Find ŏ for short / o /. Find the example word: **fox**.

Find / aw / on the **Vowel Chart**. Find the example word: **dog**.

Word Recognition and Spelling

We put consonants and vowels together to make words. Every English word has at least one vowel.

These examples use Unit 5 sound-spelling correspondences.

> **Examples: Unit Words**
> **boss, off, doll, fizz**

Some words are made up of two or more smaller words. These are called **compound words**. In a compound word, both words have to be real words that can stand alone.

> **Example: Compound Word**
> **hill + top = hilltop**

Read these Unit 5 compound words.

backdrop	hilltop
backlog	hotdog
backstop	jackpot
bobcat	laptop
cannot	windmill

Syllables: Words are made up of parts, called syllables.

- Some words have just one syllable.
- Every syllable has one vowel sound.
- A syllable may or may not be a word by itself.
- A two-syllable word may or may not be a compound word.

Read these Unit 5 two-syllable words. They have the VC/CV pattern.

VC/CV

bobbin	coffin	cosmic	mascot
classic	combat	goblin	nonfat

Some two-syllable words have a different pattern.

> **Example: VC/V**
>
> rob + in = robin
>
> vc + v = vc/v

Read these Unit 5 two-syllable words with the VC/V pattern.

VC/V

cabin	limit	rabid	topic
clinic	livid	rapid	tropic
comic	manic	robin	valid
critic	mimic	static	visit
frolic	panic	timid	vivid
habit	profit	tonic	

Essential Words

here, there, these, those, where, why

At the ends of one-syllable words, after a short vowel, $/s/$, $/f/$, $/l/$, and $/z/$ are usually represented by double letters **-ss**, **-ff**, **-ll**, **-zz**.

Use double letters -**ss**, -**ff**, -**ll**, -**zz**:

- At the end of words
- After one short vowel
- In many one-syllable words

> **Examples:** Words With Double Letters
> pass, stiff, will, jazz

Spelling Lists: The Unit 5 spelling lists contain three word categories:

1. Words that use **o** to spell short / o / or / aw /

2. Words that end with -**ss**, -**ff**, -**ll**, or -**zz**

3. **Essential Words** (in italics)

Spelling Lists

Lessons 1—5		Lessons 6—10	
cross	*those*	boss	jazz
here	top	cabin	off
lock	*where*	cannot	profit
there	*why*	classic	rock
these	will	critic	visit

Vocabulary and Morphology

Unit Vocabulary: Sound-spelling correspondences from this and previous units make up this unit's vocabulary.

- What do these words mean?
- Do some of them mean more than one thing? Which ones?
- Note: *On* is listed both in the top section and bottom section of the Unit Vocabulary box. *Both* pronunciations are correct.

UNIT Vocabulary

-ss, -ff, -ll, -zz, o for short /o/

bill	flock	lock	rot
block	font	lot	sill
blond	gill	mill	smog
blot	glass	miss	sniff
bond	golf	mob	sock
cannot	got	mop	spill
class	grass	nod	spot
clock	grill	not	stiff
crop	hill	odd	still
dock	hop	on	stock
doll	hot	pass	stop
dot	ill	pill	top
drill	jazz	pop	will
drop	job	pot	
fill	kill	rob	
fizz	kiss	rock	

o for / aw /

boss	dog	log	on
cost	frog	lost	soft
cross	frost	off	

Idiomatic Expressions Review: An **idiomatic expression**, or idiom, is a common phrase that cannot be understood by the meanings of its separate words—only by the entire phrase.

> **Examples: Idiomatic Expressions**
>
> **pass the hat** = take up a collection of money
>
> **hit the spot** = be exactly right; be refreshing
>
> **fill the bill** = serve a particular purpose

Word Relationships: Words have **attributes** such as size, parts, color, and function. Attributes refine meaning and build associations.

> **Examples: Attributes**
>
> Size: She lost the **big** stamp.
>
> Parts: Fish have **gills**.
>
> Color: He has a **green** truck.
>
> Function: A clock **tells time**.

Meaning Parts

- **Review:** Adding **-s** also signals the person and tense of the verb: **-s** means present tense (he nods, she stops, the top of the can pops).

- Adding **-ing** to a verb means ongoing action. When used with **am**, **is**, or **are**, it means ongoing action in the present. (See Step 4: Grammar and Usage.)

  > **Examples: Ongoing Action**
  > He **is picking** apples.

Grammar and Usage

Verbs describe action. Verbs also show time. If something is happening now, it is the **present tense**.

- The **-s** at the end of verbs signals present tense: **he hops, she drops, it stops**.

- The ending **-ing** at the end of verbs also signals ongoing action: he **is hopping**, they **are dropping**.

Tense Timeline

Yesterday	Today	Tomorrow
Past	Present	Future
	-s	
	-ing	

Read these Unit 5 verbs. Repeat each one, and add **-ing**.

Verbs			
bill	drill	jog	rob
block	drop	lock	sniff
clock	fill	mob	spill
clog	golf	mock	spot
cross	grill	nod	stop
dock	hop	prompt	wilt

Review: Adverbs are an English word class.

- Adverbs have several jobs. One job is to describe verbs.

- Adverbs can be single words (daily, suddenly, then).

- Some prepositional phrases behave like adverbs. They begin with a preposition and end with a noun (on Monday, in the house, to the class).

- Adverbs and prepositional phrases that act as adverbs tell **when**, **where**, or **how**.

The **predicate** of the sentence contains information about the verb, including answers to the questions **when**, **where**, or **how**.

Words or phrases that answer these questions can be moved within the sentence.

> **Examples: Phrases**
>
> Julio fed the horse **at night**.
>
> **At night**, Julio fed the horse.

Mechanics: Commas are used to signal a pause when reading or writing to clarify meaning. Commas are used to set off phrases at the beginning of sentences.

> **Examples: Phrases With Commas**
>
> At the end of the song, Jim clapped.
>
> Yesterday, school was cancelled.

The diagram below shows how to build a sentence with a subject, predicate, and adverb (or prepositional phrase that acts as an adverb).

Form: ADV/N/V   adverb/noun/verb

Function: ADV/S/P   adverb/subject/predicate

Then the class clapped.

adverb / subject; noun / predicate;
action verb

At the end, the class clapped.

adverb / subject; noun / predicate;
action verb

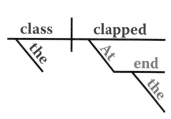

Listening and Reading

We read different kinds of text.

- **Expository** text provides information. In informational text, we listen and read for the topic and details that support that topic. Details include ideas and facts.

- **Narrative** text tells a story. When we read a story, we listen or look for the parts of a story: characters, setting, events, and resolution.

Knowing the kind of text helps us focus on the right kind of information. When we focus on the right kind of information, we understand the text.

STEP 6

Speaking and Writing

We use different types of sentences when we speak and write.

Some sentences present facts or opinions. These are called statements.

> **Examples: Statements**
>
> **Jazz is fantastic.** This tells us an opinion about jazz.
>> What? It is fantastic.
>
> **Louis Armstrong played jazz.** This tells us a fact about Louis Armstrong.
>> What? He played jazz.
>
> **Scat is part of jazz.** This tells us a fact about scat.
>> What? It is part of jazz.

Some sentences ask for information. These are called questions. Questions beginning with **where** require a place in the answer.

> **Examples: Questions**
>
> **Where** did she run? She ran on the track.
>> *On the track* tells **where** she ran.
>
> **Where** did it snow? It snowed in Wisconsin.
>> *In Wisconsin* tells **where** it snowed.

Questions beginning with **why** require a reason or explanation in the answer.

> **Example: Question**
>
> **Why** was the game cancelled?
>> Due to snow, the game was cancelled.
>> *Due to snow* tells **why** the game was cancelled.

More About Words

Expand vocabulary by learning these Bonus Words. Bonus Words use the same sound-spelling correspondences that we have studied in this unit and previous units.

UNIT Bonus Words

ascot	cop	handbill	mom	slot
backdrop	cosmic	hilltop	moss	smock
backlog	cot	hiss	nonfat	snob
backstop	crisscross	hock	opt	sob
bass	critic	hog	panic	sod
bliss	dill	hotdog	plod	staff
bobbin	dog tag	inhibit	plop	static
bobcat	don	jackpot	plot	stockings
brass	flop	jock	pod	stomp
cabin	floss	jog	pond	till
cliff	fog	jot	prod	timid
clinic	fond	lapdog	profit	tonic
clog	frill	limit	prom	topic
clot	frizz	livid	prompt	toss
cob	frock	lob	prop	trill
cod	frolic	loft	rabid	trod
coffin	frond	loss	rapid	tropic
cog	glob	manic	robin	trot
combat	gloss	mascot	rod	valid
comic	goblin	mimic	romp	visit
comic strip	gobs	mock	skill	vivid
con	habit	mod	slop	windmill

Idiom	Meaning
at the drop of a hat	immediately and without urging
be on to	be aware of or have information about
fill the bill	serve a particular purpose
hit the jackpot	win; have success
hit the spot	be exactly right; be refreshing
pass the hat	take up a collection of money
tilt at windmills	confront and engage in conflict with an imagined opponent or threat

Why? Word History

Jazz—Some say the word *jazz* comes from the name of an African American Chicago musician, Jasbo Brown, who played early jazz. A famous jazz musician, Jelly Roll Morton, claimed that he invented the word in 1902. A sportswriter, Scoop Gleeson, used the word in 1914 to mean active and lively. After that, *jazz* came to mean the music itself.

What Is Jazz?

Relax, kick back, and discover jazz. Jazz reminds us of our past and jazz still lives today.

TEACHER: Music is a language of its own. It has a written code and recognized, meaningful symbols. Jazz is a kind of music.

STUDENT: **What is jazz?**

TEACHER: Jazz is a type or kind of music. There are many kinds of music. You might be more familiar with rock or rap. What are jazz, rock, and rap?

STUDENT: **Jazz is music. Rock is music. Rap is music.**

TEACHER: While music is a language, it is not spoken. It is a language that is played or sung. How is this language of music communicated?

STUDENT: **It is played. It is sung.**

TEACHER: How did jazz begin? Many styles of music have their roots in classical music. Composers of classical music wrote very specific note sequences for musicians to play. Composers wrote or drafted their music on special paper. How do composers write their music?

STUDENT: **They draft it.**

TEACHER: How does jazz differ from this classical style of music? The difference has to do with how the musician uses written music. Musicians of classical music play the music exactly as it is written. They place their sheets of music on a stand. Where do musicians keep their music?

STUDENT: **It is on a stand.**

TEACHER: With jazz, they don't play the music exactly as it is written. When jazz musicians play their songs, they often add notes that are not written down. This is called improvising or "jamming." A "jam session" is where musicians create new music or add to existing music as they play. How are musicians of classical music different from jazz musicians?

STUDENT: **They stick to the written music. Jazz bands do not.**

TEACHER: People who prefer jazz might have criticized classical music for being so rigid. What did they say about classical music?

STUDENT: **Critics said it was strict. The critics pick jazz.**

TEACHER: Classical music was written hundreds of years ago and yet it is still popular today. It is a music form that has endured. When something holds its value over time, we consider it a classic. What can be said about this enduring style of music?

STUDENT: **It is classic!**

TEACHER: Say this sentence another way: The impact of this classical style of music has been incredible.

STUDENT: **It has had an impact. The impact is fantastic!**

TEACHER: For example, current music styles such as rock, rap, and hip-hop have been influenced by classical music. Name several styles of music that have been influenced by classical music.

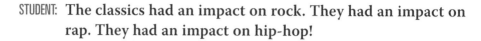

STUDENT: The classics had an impact on rock. They had an impact on rap. They had an impact on hip-hop!

TEACHER: Over time, other traditional music forms or styles developed to reflect people's daily lives. Consider what some of these styles might be.

STUDENT: What is on the list?

TEACHER: Six kinds of traditional music are on the list. These styles of music formed the foundation for jazz. Where do we get the musical strands that led to the development of jazz?

STUDENT: The past gives the strands.

TEACHER: The six types of music include: church music, work songs, minstrel shows, ballads, ragtime, and the blues. Jazz is an American music form that has evolved from many different kinds of music. How does music from the past affect jazz?

STUDENT: Music from the past impacts jazz.

TEACHER: Work songs were a natural development. These songs helped make the long day in the fields pass more rapidly. The work was difficult. The rhythm or beat of the music served as a prompt to help them work together. Tell me about the role of work songs.

STUDENT: Digging was a hot, drab task. Picking crops was a hot job. They did the tasks to music. They were glad to have it. They got the crops in fast.

TEACHER: In ballads, music was simply the format for storytelling. While many ballads were based on real people and real events, details were added that were not necessarily true. What can you tell me about a ballad?

STUDENT: **It is a story. The facts are not valid.**

TEACHER: Church was very important for people who had very few possessions and privileges. It was where they went to give thanks and receive comfort. Passionate music filled the church and became their offering when they had no money to give. What do some churchgoers give instead of money?

STUDENT: **They give a gift. It is music.**

TEACHER: Minstrel shows were an early form of entertainment. They included musical numbers, short plays, and comedy routines or skits. The audience participated by clapping their hands and stomping their feet. Tell me what you know about a minstrel show.

STUDENT: **It has music. It has skits. It has slapstick. The fans stomp. They clap for the band.**

TEACHER: The performers in a play are called the cast. The cast of performers in a minstrel show would often sing and wear top hats. Describe the performers.

STUDENT: **The cast had on top hats.**

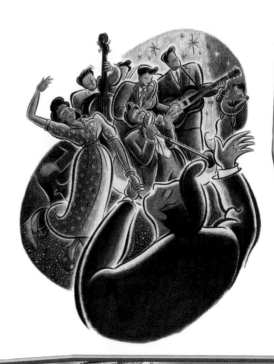

TEACHER: Ragtime music was also very popular. It was lively and loud. Pianos were an essential element. People liked dancing to ragtime. What do you know about ragtime music?

STUDENT: **It is fast. It is brisk. Fans spin. They kick to the music.**

TEACHER: "The blues" reflected the darker side of life. These performers knew many hardships and put them in their music. Paraphrase this statement: "Their difficult past forms the background for the music."

STUDENT: **The backdrop is a sad past.**

TEACHER: When they played their songs, they often added notes that were not written down. When musicians improvise or take liberty with the music, they "ad-lib." This style of music is still very popular today. It is very "relaxed" or "kicked back." Tell me what you know about the blues.

STUDENT: **Bands ad-lib. They kick back and jam.**

TEACHER: Jazz has its origins in work songs, church music, ballads, minstrel shows, ragtime, and the blues. What has become of these old styles of music?

STUDENT: **In jazz, the past is not lost. The strands live on. What impact did they have?**

TEACHER: The mixture of musical elements created jazz. Paraphrase the following sentence: "Jazz is a new form of music."

STUDENT: **Jazz adds a new twist.**

TEACHER: Jazz was extremely popular in the 1920s. This period was known as the Jazz Age. People flocked to hear jazz played. They listened and danced to the music. How can you describe jazz in the early years?

STUDENT: **Jazz is a hit. Fans flock to it.**

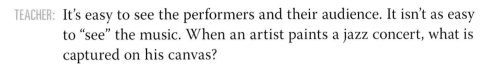

TEACHER: It's easy to see the performers and their audience. It isn't as easy to "see" the music. When an artist paints a jazz concert, what is captured on his canvas?

STUDENT: **It has the band. It has the fans. It has the music.**

TEACHER: Loud, colorful, strong lines help you imagine the music and the mood. The art captures the music on the canvas. It creates a visual texture that matches the music. How would you describe this art?

STUDENT: **It is vivid. The art is abstract. It gives jazz a "fabric." Its fabric is abstract.**

TEACHER: In the early days of photography, bands being photographed had to sit perfectly still for at least a minute. With faster film, such posing for a picture was no longer necessary. Pictures could be as spontaneous or candid as the music. What was it like to have a picture made in the 1920s?

STUDENT: **The band had to sit still. The film was not fast. It was not candid.**

TEACHER: Artists and photographers have created a visual history of jazz. They have captured the mood or feeling of the music in concrete and abstract ways. What element gives these pictures and photographs their spark?

STUDENT: **It is jazz. Its fabric is vivid.**

TEACHER: Jazz is truly an American music form. It has its roots in the past, yet it has endured. Its popularity continues today. Summarize the selection.

STUDENT: **Jazz is the topic. The past lives in jazz. The fabric of jazz is vivid. Jazz is still a hit. It is not a fad. In fact, it's a new classic!**

Jazz: The Recipe

recipe

the directions and ingredients to make something; a formula

How did jazz begin? There was a **recipe**! There were many parts. There were different people. There were Africans. There were Europeans. There was different music. There was the blues. There was ragtime. All of
5 these combined. They made up the recipe. America's own music was born. It was **jazz**.

Workers sang. Where? They sang in fields. They sang on ships. They sang on railroads. The **work song** was a part of their day. People worked together. They sang
10 work songs. They worked to a beat. The songs made it easier. There were many kinds of work songs. Work songs played a part in jazz.

Church music was important to jazz. African Americans made new kinds of church music. Black
15 people formed churches. They rewrote old songs. They changed words. They changed the beat. They changed

the tune. They used the old " **call and response** ." They sang in the old way. But the music was new. This music played a part in jazz.

20   White Americans added to jazz. The Scotch-Irish had **ballads**. These were much loved. Ballads tell a story. They tell of bravery. They tell of heroes. They tell sad stories. They retell old stories. They tell new ones. In a ballad, the words are important. They are more

25 important than the music. Ballads played a part in jazz.

    Minstrel shows played a part in jazz. These shows were popular. We might call them variety shows. There was singing. There was dancing. There was comedy. There were black performers. There were white

30 performers.

    Dance music was popular. **Plantations** held dances. They were big events. Bands played. Musicians had jobs. Many slaves learned to play. They played fiddles. They played flutes. They invented the banjo.

35 Black musicians learned the songs. They played the tunes in the evening. They changed them a bit. African and European music combined. Dance music played a part in jazz.

    The 1800s came along. A new kind of music was

40 born. It was loud and fun. Pianos pounded. It was called **ragtime**. All the musicians played it. They played in dance halls. The tunes were good. The words were good. Everybody loved ragtime. It had strong beats. It had catchy tunes. It was lively. It was

45 surprising. Ragtime played a part in jazz.

    When were the **blues** first played? They were played sometime in the late 1800s. Slaves were free. Still, life was hard. People were sad. They were frustrated. They showed their feelings in music. They called it the blues.

50 Today, people still sing the blues when they're sad. The blues played a part in jazz.

    The recipe came together. Where? In **New Orleans** ! By 1890, New Orleans was America's music city. It

opera

a performance where the story is set to music

Mardi Gras

a holiday marked by parades and carnivals

had **opera**. It had concerts. It had ballrooms. It had
55 parades. It had the **Mardi Gras**! Many different people
lived there. There were Africans. There were Native
Americans. There were French. There were Spanish.
There were people from everywhere. Together, they
created America's own music. **Jazz**.

Adapted from "Jazz Ingredients"
by Heather Mitchell Amey

Answer It
Say the answer in a complete sentence.

1. Where did people sing work songs?

2. What kind of music added to the recipe for jazz?

3. What did African Americans do to change church music?

4. What stories do ballads tell?

5. Why were minstrel shows called variety shows?

6. Why were freed slaves singing the blues?

7. Where were dances held?

8. What did slaves learn to play?

9. When was ragtime born?

10. What kind of music included pianos?

Photograph ©2004 Museum of Fine Arts, Boston

Looking at Jazz

We *hear* jazz. But can we *see* it? Some have tried. Artists have captured jazz. The music is alive. Some can catch its spirit. They show people. They show them playing. They show them dancing. They use color.
5 They use line. They *show* jazz. They show the **mood**. They show the feeling.

It was the Jazz Age. Go back to the 1920s. Jazz was *it*. It was like rock and rap today. Kids loved it. It was more than popular. It was the *in thing*. The '20s were
10 new. They were special. How? People felt alive. They felt free. They had fun. Jazz! Flappers! What were flappers? They were young women. They loved jazz.

mood
the feeling or impression created

They loved dancing to jazz. Artists loved to paint them dancing.

15   Sometimes, artists changed things. They changed what they saw. They changed the look of things. They used strange lines. They used **bold** colors. The colors made moods. They used different lines. Curved lines are restful. Zigzag lines are nervous. Black is gloomy.
20 Red is exciting. Artists changed the colors. They changed the scenes. They got the mood. They got the feeling. They painted jazz.

    Music **inspires** art. You can spot these pictures. They *look* like jazz. They look like the music. They
25 have **rhythm** . They have color. They have strong lines.

bold
easily seen; flashy

inspires
causes or provokes

rhythm
a uniform pattern of colors, lines, and shapes

abstraction
an artistic piece that doesn't look like the real object

Photograph ©2004 Museum of Fine Arts, Boston

Hot Still Scape With Six Colors— Seventh Avenue Style

Hot Still Scape With Six Colors— Seventh Avenue Style is a jazzy title.

It is an **abstraction** by Stuart Davis, an American artist. Stuart often said that the spirit of jazz inspired all of his art.

    Photographers captured jazz, too. Photography got better. First, film was faster. Then, flash became portable. This was important. Photographers could work at the shows. They could take pictures of jazz.
30 They'd find the right angle. They'd wait for the right moment. Then, they'd snap!

Artists have caught the jazz feeling. Jazz can be pictures. They are loud. They are strong. They are lively. They are **distinct**. They are like the music. They

35 *are* jazz!

distinct
clearly different; individual

Adapted from "Looking at Jazz" by Marc H. Miller

Lisette Model's photograph of Louis Armstrong performing at the Newport Jazz Festival looks simple. But it was the result of hard work. It took careful calculation and quick reflexes.

Louis Armstrong performs at the Newport Jazz Festival. Photographed by Lisette Model.

©Lisette Model Estate: National Portrait Gallery, Smithsonian Institution/Art Resource, NY

Answer It
Say the answer in a complete sentence.

1. What do pictures of jazz show?

2. When was the Jazz Age?

3. Why did artists use strange lines and unusual colors?

4. How does music inspire art?

5. Why did artists take or draw jazz pictures?

6. Why were the 1920s remembered for jazz?

7. What did artists change when they painted pictures?

8. Why did artists use black and red in their paintings?

9. Why did artists use zigzag and curved lines?

Growing Up With Jazz

"When I was a kid, I would rather do without food than without music." Who said that? The person who dominated the jazz world for half a century. Louis Armstrong. Satchmo. The most beloved jazzman who
5 ever lived.

On August 4, 1901, Louis was born in New Orleans. In New Orleans, people said that Louis and jazz were born together. Louis said it himself. "Jazz and I grew up side by side." He lived in a home without electricity.
10 There was no plumbing. Louis' father left the family when Louis was a baby. Times were hard.

By the fifth grade, Louis left school. He hit the streets. He looked for ways to earn money. He peddled

newspapers. He delivered buckets of coal from a mule-
15 drawn wagon. With his earnings, his mother could
buy food and cook. Louis loved the red beans and rice
the people of New Orleans still love today. Most of
all, Louis loved listening to the bands that played in
parades and funerals. Recalling those days, Armstrong
20 later commented, "Even the pie man used to play
something on the **bugle** . The waffle man rang a big
triangle. The junk man had one of them long tin horns.
In New Orleans, there was always something that was
nice, and always with music." Louis himself sang on
25 street corners with a group of friends. He was with
friends when he got into bad trouble.

bugle
a trumpet-shaped
horn without keys

It was New Year's Eve. Louis was about 13 years old.
He wanted to have some fun and impress his friends.
From a street corner, he fired a pistol he had taken
30 from his stepfather. He was arrested. Louis was sent to
the Colored **Waifs**' Home, a reform school. Amazingly,
Louis "took to it." For the first time, he had regular
meals and clean clothes. Best of all, the home had a
marching band. Louis learned to play the trumpet!
35 Within a year, he proudly led the band through his old
neighborhood.

waifs
abandoned
children; orphans

When he got out, Louis spent his days hauling coal.
He spent his nights in the honky-tonks, begging for
a chance to sit in with a band. Years passed before he
40 had a job in a dance hall.

In 1922, Armstrong received a **telegram** from
Chicago ordering him to "come immediately. I have
a job for you in my band." It was from his old friend
and mentor, the famous "King" Oliver. With a few
45 dollars in his pocket, his horn, and a fish sandwich,
he took the train to Chicago. In Chicago, Armstrong
met Lillian Hardin, the young pianist in King Oliver's
band. She and Armstrong were married in 1924, with
Lil determined to make him "believe in himself" and
50 strike out on his own.

telegram
a message sent
by a code-making
machine

With Lil's encouragement, his career took off. He made some of his most famous records during the 1920s. He became the idol of jazz musicians. He played in legendary bands in Chicago and New York. He
55 toured Europe, where, much to his surprise, his records had already made him famous.

Increasingly, Louis became a show business entertainer. He appeared on **Broadway**. He was featured on radio programs and in the movies. He enjoyed fame.
60 He reveled in the applause of his adoring audiences. He returned to his home in New Orleans to become King Zulu on Mardi Gras day. To this day, he is the most beloved son of Louis' hometown. The New Orleans airport is named for Louis. Armstrong Park sits in the
65 middle of New Orleans, an honor to his memory.

Louis overcame poverty and prejudice. He became the most famous jazz musician in the world. When he died in 1971 in New York City, 25,000 people came to pay their respects. Together, Louis and jazz made a
70 permanent mark on American culture.

Adapted from "Growing Up With Jazz"
by Carol Gelber

Broadway

famous theater district in New York City

Scat and **Improvisation**

What makes jazz jazz? Scat. Improvisation. Where did they come from? Some say that one day Louis Armstrong forgot the words to the song his band was recording. That accident helped to make him famous and helped make
75 jazz jazz.

It was 1926. Louis' band, The Hot Five, was recording. The tune was "Heebie Jeebies," a song about a popular dance. Louis sang the first verse as it was written. "I got the heebies, I mean the jeebies . . .
80 come on and do that dance they call the heebie jeebies dance." When he got to the second verse, he sang,

improvisation

creating music as it is being played

"Deep-dah-jeep-bop-a-dobby-oh-doe-dah, leep-a-la-da-dee-da-dee-oh-bo."

The story goes that he had dropped the sheet music
85 and could not remember the words. He did not want
to spoil the master. (The master was the wax cylinder
used to press recordings.) So he made up sounds to go
along with the music!

Armstrong did not invent this kind of singing,
90 called *scat*, but he was one of the first to record it.
People loved the funny song. It sold 40,000 copies in
just a few weeks. (This was more than many early
records sold in their lifetime.) His records and
performances became more and more popular. Jazz
95 fans were fascinated with the way Armstrong could
play around with words and music. Other musicians
imitated him, and Louis' style—improvisation—
became an element of jazz.

Adapted from "Scat and Improvisation"
by Virginia A. Spatz

Think About It

1. What city was the home of Louis Armstrong?

2. What two ways did Louis earn money as a child in New Orleans?

3. What might have happened to Louis' life if he had not been sent to reform school?

4. After Louis Armstrong became famous he returned to New Orleans, his home town. Why do you think he returned? Do you think you will visit the place where you grew up when you are an adult? Why or why not?

5. What accident helped to make Louis Armstrong famous?

6. When Louis Armstrong forgot the words to the song he was singing, he chose to continue by singing nonsensical words. Why do you think he chose to continue rather than quitting?

THE DUKE JAZZES NEWPORT

It was the last night. The 1956 Newport Jazz Festival was ending. The Duke Ellington **Orchestra** came on stage. It was around midnight. People were beginning to leave. Ellington growled, "What are we, the animal act,
5 the acrobats?" He referred to the old days. Back then, less important acts closed shows, as the audience left.

Ellington's fame had faded. Great jazz musicians had come and gone. Pop, bebop, and rock and roll had replaced them. Ellington's music was out of fashion. Nightclubs had
10 closed; record sales had plummeted. In 1949, one music critic had asked, "Isn't it about time the Ellington orchestra was **disbanded**?" The Duke was one of the greatest musicians of the century. He felt **devastated**.

The band played several numbers that night. At
15 last, Ellington turned from the **piano**. He called for "Diminuendo and Crescendo in Blue." He had first recorded this one in 1937. The band started playing. Paul Gonsalves stood. He had his **tenor saxophone**. He made his way to the front. Duke encouraged him from the
20 piano. Jo Jones sat in front. Jo was the drummer for Count Basie, another jazz great. Jo cheered Gonsalves on. He beat the rhythm with a newspaper.

Gonsalves played. He played over the band's rhythm. He played softly. Then he grew louder. People sat up
25 straighter. Excitement rippled through the crowd. Hot jazz notes soared. The night was electric. Everybody began to clap. People shouted. Some danced in the aisles. Soon, everyone was standing. Gonsalves "blew the joint down." They lasted for 27 **choruses**.
30 Photographers ran here and there. They tried to capture the mood. The place was wild. The crowd was wound up. Some feared a riot. One man asked Ellington to stop. They kept right on playing. The band played for 90 minutes that night. They left the audience buzzing.
35 *Down Beat* magazine reported it. "The final night of the 1956 Newport Jazz Festival will not soon be forgotten.

orchestra
a group of musicians playing different instruments

disbanded
stopped functioning as a group; broke up

devastated
extremely upset

piano
a large musical instrument with a keyboard

tenor saxophone
a wind instrument that plays a lower range of notes

choruses
sections of a song played repeatedly

Some fans were smart enough to stay until the end."
The Duke's picture made the cover of *Time.* The picture
showed what the music world already knew: Duke
40 Ellington was back.

Adapted from "Making a Statement at Newport"
by Brandon Marie Miller

Think About It

1. What happened when Duke Ellington's band came on stage?

2. This article says that by 1956, the great jazz musicians had come and gone. What had been the replacements of jazz?

3. What instrument did Paul Gonsalves play in Ellington's band?

4. As Paul Gonsalves played, "excitement rippled through the crowd." What other kinds of events can cause similar excitement in an audience?

5. One man asked Ellington to stop playing because he feared a riot. Defend Ellington's decision to continue playing. Do you think this was a good decision? Why or why not?

6. Explain how you think Duke Ellington felt when he went on stage at the 1956 Newport Jazz Festival. How did he feel when he left the stage that night?

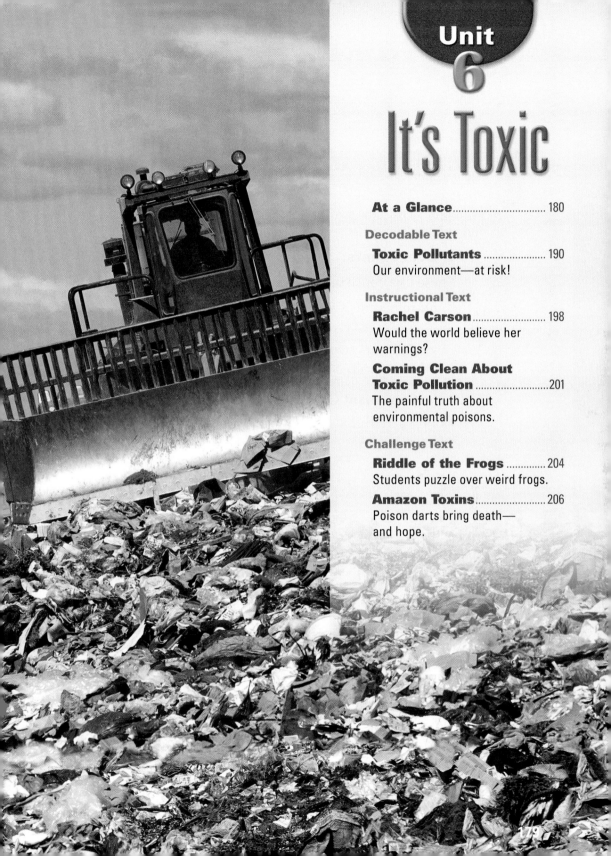

STEP 1

Phonemic Awareness and Phonics

Unit 6 has two new consonants, **q** and **x**. In English spelling, **q** is followed by **u**.

■ **Consonants:**

These two consonants, **q** and **x**, have unique spelling patterns:

qu represents two phonemes: / k / + / w / (quit / *kwit* /; quack / *kwak* /; quill / *kwil* /).

x represents two phonemes: / k / + / s / (tax / *taks* /; mix / *miks* /).

Go to the **Consonant Chart** on page 209. Find the sounds for **qu** and **x** on the chart.

STEP 2

Word Recognition and Spelling

We put vowels and consonants together to make words. Every English word has at least one vowel.

> **Examples: Unit Words**
>
> **quit, tax, mix**

Some words are made up of two or more smaller words or syllables.

Read these Unit 6 two-syllable words. These have the VC/VC pattern.

VC/VC

axis	toxic	toxin

These are Unit 6 compound words.

hatbox	quicksand
hotbox	sandbox

Essential Words

down, for, her, how, me, now

Spelling: The Doubling Rule

When a

- one-syllable word
- with one vowel
- ends in one consonant

double the final consonant *before* adding a suffix beginning with a vowel.

> **Example: Doubling Rule: Suffix With Vowel**
>
> **hop + ing = hopping**

Do not double the consonant when the suffix begins with a consonant.

> **Example: Doubling Rule: Suffix With Consonant**
>
> **cap + ful = capful**

This is also called the **1-1-1 Rule**:

1 syllable

1 vowel

1 consonant at the end

Spelling Lists: The Unit 6 spelling lists contain two word categories:

1. Words with the new vowel sounds spelled **qu** and **x**

2. Essential Words (in italics)

Spelling Lists

Lessons 1–5		Lessons 6–10	
down	*me*	axis	quitting
for	*now*	fix	sandbox
fox	quack	quicksand	toxic
her	quick	quilt	toxins
how	six	quints	wax

STEP

3 Vocabulary and Morphology

Unit Vocabulary: Sound-spelling correspondences from this unit and previous units make up this unit's vocabulary.

- What do these words mean?

- Do some of them mean more than one thing? Which ones?

UNIT Vocabulary

qu, x			
box	mix	quilt	toxic
fix	quack	six	toxins
fox	quick	tax	wax

Idiomatic Expressions Review: An **idiomatic expression**, or idiom, is a common phrase that cannot be understood by the meanings of its separate words—only by the entire phrase.

Examples: Idiomatic Expressions

at the drop of a hat = immediately and without urging

pat on the back = congratulate; encourage someone

be on to = be aware of or have information about

Word Relationships Review:

- Words that have opposite meanings are **antonyms**. Think of opposites for the **Unit Vocabulary** words.

- Words that have the same or similar meaning are **synonyms**. Examples: big/huge; quick/fast; fix/repair. Think of synonyms for the **Unit Vocabulary** words.

- Words have **attributes**, such as size, parts, color, and function.

Meaning Parts

- Adding letters or punctuation to words can change or add meanings.
- **Review:** Two verb endings can signal the present.

  -**s**   Examples: He **quits**. She **quilts**. It **quacks**.
         (right now)

  -**ing**   Examples: He is **quitting**. They are **quacking**.
         (ongoing action)

STEP 4

Grammar and Usage

Review: Pronouns are function words used in place of nouns. Different groups of pronouns have different functions.

Nominative (subject) **pronouns** (**I, you, he, she, it, we, you, they**) take the place of the subject in a sentence.

Other pronouns take the place of objects. They are called **objective pronouns**. **Me, you, him, her, it, us**, and **them** are objective pronouns.

> **Examples: Objective Pronouns**
> The teacher helped **them**.
> Carla is handing the plant to **her**.

Review: Prepositions are function words. They show the position or relationship to nouns or pronouns.

Most prepositions show a position in

- space (inside, over, under)
- time (during, since, until)
- space and time (after, from, through)

Adjectives describe nouns.

- They answer: **which one**, **how many**, and **what kind**.
- They can be single words (six, new) or phrases (from the school).
- Some prepositional phrases act like adjectives. These phrases begin with a preposition and end with a noun.

> **Example: Adjectives**
>
> **Six new** kids **from the school** won the big game.
> | | |
> |---|---|
> | How many? | six |
> | What kind? | new |
> | Which ones? | from the school |

The subject of the sentence can include adjectives describing the person, place, thing, or idea (noun) that the sentence is about. For example:

How many?	**Six** students went to the game.
What kind?	The **new** players dressed for the game.
Which one?	The team **from their school** won the game.

The diagram below shows the relationship of the adjective to the subject.

Form: ADJ/N/V   **adjective/noun/verb**
Function: ADJ/S/P   **adjective/subject/predicate**

Six **students went.**

adjective; **noun / verb**

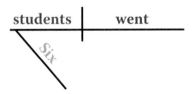

5 Listening and Reading

We read different kinds of text.

- **Expository** text provides information. In informational text, we listen and read for the topic and details that support that topic. Details include ideas and facts.

- **Narrative** text tells a story. When we read a story, we listen or look for the parts of a story: characters, setting, events, and resolution.

Knowing the type of text helps us focus on the right kind of information. When we focus on the right kind of information, we understand the text.

Speaking and Writing

We use different types of sentences when we speak and write.

Some sentences present facts or opinions. These are called statements.

> **Examples: Statements**
>
> **Toxins can make you sick.** This tells us a fact about toxins.
>
> What? They can make you sick.
>
> **Rachel Carson studied pollution.** This tells us a fact about Rachel Carson.
>
> What? She studied pollution.

Some sentences ask for information. These are called questions. Questions beginning with **how** require answers that tell how something is done or happens.

> **Examples: Questions**
>
> **How** did he run? He ran fast. *Fast* tells **how** he ran.
>
> **How** did they do it? They did it as a class. *As a class* tells how they did it.

More About Words

Expand vocabulary by learning these Bonus Words. Bonus Words use the same sound-spelling correspondences that we have studied in this unit and previous units.

UNIT Bonus Words

ax	hatbox	pox	quints	sandbox
axis	hotbox	quicksand	quip	sax
fax	lax	quid	quit	sox
flax	nix	quill	quiz	toxin

Why? Word History

Toxic and Toxin—The English words, *toxic* and *toxin*, come from an Old Persian word that sounded something like *tocksha* and meant "arrow." The Greeks changed the word to *toxikon*, which meant "poison for arrows." Later, the Romans borrowed the word from the Greeks. They changed it to *toxicum*, which in Latin meant "poison." English borrowed the word from Latin. Today, *toxin* means a poisonous substance. *Toxic* means relating to, or caused by, a harmful substance.

Toxic Pollutants

**Toxic pollution is everywhere. What can we do about it?
Rachel Carson raised awareness about toxic pollution.
Maybe you can too.**

TEACHER: Let's pretend to interview, or have a conversation with, a famous person. This individual was one of the first people to realize the effects of pesticides on our land. Let's have our guest introduce herself.

STUDENT: **I am Miss Rachel Carson.**

TEACHER: Miss Carson, I understand you were born and raised on a farm. Your mom and dad had 65 acres in the state of Pennsylvania. You must have had quite a time exploring nature.

STUDENT: **The plot of land was vast.**

TEACHER: I know that you studied hard in school. How did you learn so much about nature and the land around you if the information wasn't in your books?

STUDENT: **I had to ask mom.**

TEACHER: What were some of the things you learned from your mom?

STUDENT: **I got facts about rabbits and rats. We got to track them in the plants. In the pond, we could spot bass and frogs.**

TEACHER: When your mom asked what you wanted to be when you grow up, do you remember what you told her? You said . . . ?

STUDENT: **I plan to be a writer.**

TEACHER: I understand you enjoyed magazines as a youngster. In fact, your first article was published in the magazine *St. Nicholas*. This first article came from stories your older brother told you about his experiences in the war. Once you submitted the story, you didn't hear from the publisher for over a year. What did you keep telling yourself?

STUDENT: **They will print the facts about combat.**

TEACHER: What did your mom tell you would happen if your story were published?

STUDENT: **I will win a grant.**

TEACHER: When you went to college, you didn't have as much money as some of the other girls. You made up excuses when they asked you to go places with them.

STUDENT: **I admit I did.**

TEACHER: But you loved your college classes, especially biology and English. You had a memorable experience on one of your biology field trips when your teacher taught you to split apart layers of rock. Can you tell us how you found a fossil of a fish?

STUDENT: **I split the rock. It had the imprint in it.**

TEACHER: So you found a fossil, and that fascinated you! I believe you were surprised that you enjoyed the inside classes as much as the outdoor classes.

Carson exploring tide pools, Maine, 1955.

TEACHER: Your teacher taught you that each animal has a beautiful plan inside. You studied not only a grasshopper and a starfish, but also one additional animal. What was it?

STUDENT: **In the lab, we studied the plan in a frog.**

TEACHER: After you graduated, a friend wrote you a letter that caused you to investigate the use of pesticides. Your friend asked an important question. What question led to your research into the poisons the chemical companies were selling?

STUDENT: **What can kill robins?**

TEACHER: Your friend had found 14 dead robins in her yard after a poison, or toxin, called DDT had been sprayed to kill bugs. You researched this use of pesticides and found them harmful. What did you plan to do?

STUDENT: **I had plans to fix the impact of DDT.**

TEACHER: As your ideas became accepted, people everywhere wanted to hear you speak and wanted to get to know you better. You didn't like all this fame. Can you tell us why?

STUDENT: **I was a bit timid.**

TEACHER: But in spite of your timid personality, you felt the need to get the information out to people. How do you overcome your timidity?

STUDENT: **The facts prompted me to act.**

TEACHER: In addition, you decided to write another book. You had already published two books about the sea. The success of these books led you to a realization. What conclusion did you reach about your discovery of how harmful DDT is?

STUDENT: **I had to give the facts. I had to print them.**

TEACHER: Can you summarize some of your advice from the book that was printed?

Unhatched Ibis eggs, damaged because of DDT pesticide on the Texas Gulf.

STUDENT: **The facts must stop the quick profit from DDT. The land is vast. The cost to the land is vast. The task is to stop toxins.**

TEACHER: Many people criticized your book and said your information was false. In response to this, President John F. Kennedy asked for a special report from scientists to find out which side was right. What was the conclusion?

STUDENT: **They said toxins can kill. Toxic pollution is bad.**

TEACHER: If you could have given one last piece of advice to people in the 1960s, what would it be?

STUDENT: **We have to ban DDT and limit toxins.**

TEACHER: In this selection we will look at how some of our behaviors, both as individuals and as a population, impact this world in which we live. Our topic is toxic pollution and how it affects our planet. What is our topic?

STUDENT: **The topic is pollution. It is toxic. Toxins are bad. They impact the land. Toxins have a bad impact.**

TEACHER: Pollution is caused when people act in a careless or irresponsible way. They forget the pressing need to keep the Earth's environment clean. For example, instead of reusing and recycling items, people throw them away. These items often end up in a landfill. Landfills require more and more space. They take up land where homes could be built. They also make the surrounding land less desirable. What will happen when we have too much garbage?

STUDENT: **Landfills have a limit. They will pass the limit. Landfills will clog the land. Vast tracts of land will be bad.**

TEACHER: People need to find ways to change their behavior. Disposable products are convenient but they are not good for the environment. What can people do?

STUDENT: **They can stop. They can limit bad habits.**

TEACHER: Think of all the small things people drop every day without thinking: pop-tops, bottle caps, and drink cans. These are all examples of litter. Littering pollutes the immediate environment. Tell me three ways people litter.

STUDENT: **They drop cans. They drop pop-tops. They drop caps.**

TEACHER: When people camp out and picnic, they need to make sure they have picked up all of their trash. They need to leave the area clean and natural, just as they found it. Tell me two areas that need to be left clean.

STUDENT: Camps have to be clean. Picnic spots have to be clean.

TEACHER: Individuals and families have environmental responsibilities. Larger groups in our nation and in our world have the same responsibilities. The goods they produce are needed, but the cost to the environment must also be considered. Consumers need to make the environment a priority. What can consumers do?

STUDENT: They can act. They can insist on a clean environment.

TEACHER: One group that must answer the call to be responsible is farmers. Farmers till the land and plant our crops. What is their job?

STUDENT: They till the land. They plant crops.

TEACHER: We need the goods that farmers produce. Farmers need us to buy their produce. To make more profit, farmers use pesticides and fertilizers to make their crops grow more quickly. This puts the individual farmer at odds with the environment. Tell me about the farmer's conflict.

STUDENT: He has a conflict. It is about profit and loss.

TEACHER: Let's look at an example of how the farmer contributes to pollution. Think of a farm on a hilltop. Where is the farm?

STUDENT: It is on a hilltop.

TEACHER: Often farms are beside rivers and ponds. The soil is usually better in these areas. When a farmer fertilizes his crops, that substance ends up in the soil. Some of the fertilizer is absorbed by the plants. Some of it is washed into the river or pond by rain. What happens to the fertilizer that is not used by the plants?

STUDENT: **It spills off the hilltop. It spills into the water.**

TEACHER: When this happens, it sets off a sequence of events that causes pollution. The small green plants in the water are fertilized and grow faster than they normally would. This causes water plants to become thick on the top of the water and block light. The plants use up gases, like oxygen. Then fish, such as bass, cannot get the gases they need to live. In the end, all the bass in the lake die. Why did the bass die?

STUDENT: **The plants got oxygen. The bass did not.**

TEACHER: Pesticides are chemicals that kill bugs, and herbicides are chemicals that kill the weeds in fields. These toxins are also washed into rivers or ponds by the rain. They kill the plants and animals living in the water. Frogs, fish, and moss may die as a result. Explain how a toxic chemical affects life in and beside the water.

STUDENT: **Toxins kill frogs. Toxins kill bass. They kill moss.**

TEACHER: Paraphrase what I say. Large factories, or plants, also dump toxic chemicals into our fresh water supply. These toxins contribute to pollution in the environment.

Rainfall washes fertilizers and toxic pesticides into rivers and streams.

STUDENT: Big plants drop toxins. They drop them into the environment.

TEACHER: The final pollutant to discuss is something we take for granted every day. When we go places, our cars consume gas. Not all of the gas is used. Paraphrase this sentence: "Cars, trucks, and vans emit leftover particles as a form of pollution."

STUDENT: The gas is from traffic. Traffic gas is pollution.

TEACHER: This form of pollution is called smog. What is it?

STUDENT: It is smog.

TEACHER: Smog is like a heavy mist that hangs over a city. It pollutes the air. What is smog?

STUDENT: Smog is a toxic mist.

TEACHER: There are several ways we can begin to solve the problem of pollution. First, we need more information. Information can be provided in classes and clinics. What can we do?

STUDENT: We have clinics. Clinics can give facts.

TEACHER: Second, we need laws, or bills, that make those who pollute responsible.

STUDENT: How can we pass bills?

TEACHER: Informing the public and our lawmakers is important. Paraphrase these ideas.

STUDENT: We can insist on passing the bills. We can act. Bills can limit toxins. We can have an impact.

TEACHER: What conclusions can you draw from this selection?

STUDENT: Pollution is bad. It is toxic. Toxins impact the land.

Rachel Carson

Rachel Carson loved life. She loved her work. She was a scientist. She loved the sea. She became a writer. She wrote about the sea. She wrote about life.

World War II ended. Rachel was disturbed.
5 Spraying bothered her. People used pesticides. They sprayed insects. They sprayed weeds. Sprays killed the weeds. They killed insects. A common spray was DDT. What did spraying do? It turned out more crops. It turned out better crops. This was good. Everybody
10 knew this.

But Rachel knew something else. The sprays were not safe. We knew about the good. But what of the danger? Could the sprays harm living things? Rachel thought so. She watched. She studied. She took notes.
15 Spraying was killing harmful insects. That was good. But it killed friendly insects, too. There was something else. She noted the bees. Bees **pollinate**. Fruit trees needed bees. Plants needed bees. Spraying killed bees. There was much to be lost.
20 Some people tried to **control** nature. They wanted nature to work for us. Rachel warned them. She said not to

pollinate
to transfer pollen to fertilize seeds

control
to stop the spread of; suppress

change nature. She said changing nature was dangerous. We couldn't see the future. We couldn't tell what could happen. Rachel told us. This is what she said. "We need
25 to think of ourselves differently. The universe is vast. It is incredible. We are just a tiny part of it."

Rachel would put her warnings in writing. She would write a book. It would be a book all people could understand. She had to warn them. The danger was real.
30 She worked carefully. She checked her reports. She began writing the book. She named it *Silent Spring*. What did the title mean? It **predicted** a terrible time. It told of a spring when no birds would sing. At last, she finished the book. She knew what would happen. She knew the book
35 would be attacked. Some would disagree. Some would **criticize**. Some would even attack her. Business was involved. Money was involved. But Rachel did not quit.

Silent Spring was published in 1962. Arguments began. All over the world, people read the book. They
40 asked questions. Should we try to control nature? Or should we **protect** nature? Soon, we were working on the problem. We would learn to control pests. But we would not harm other living things. The U.S.

predicted
said in advance; foretold

criticize
to find faults or flaws in

protect
to keep safe

Rachel Carson wrote her manuscript for Silent Spring *by hand.*

agency

a government
department in
charge of certain
laws and regulations

government created an **agency**. Other countries
45 worked on the problem, too.

Rachel Carson made change happen. Her book
affected us all. In 1970, people celebrated the first
Earth Day. Everywhere, people began to think about
these things. People began to understand. Today, our
50 world is better. It is better because of Rachel.

Rachel Louise Carson

Born: *May 27, 1907, in Springdale, Pennsylvania*

Died: *April 14, 1964, in Silver Spring, Maryland*

Books: *Under the Sea-Wind (1941), The Sea Around Us (1951),*
             The Edge of the Sea (1955), Silent Spring (1962), and
             The Sense of Wonder (posthumous, 1965)

Answer It
Say the answer in a complete sentence.

1. Who is Rachel Carson?

2. What is DDT?

3. How are pesticides helpful? How are they harmful?

4. What worried Rachel?

5. How were some people changing nature?

6. Why did Rachel write the book *Silent Spring*? Why did Rachel call it *Silent Spring*?

7. In paragraph five: "She knew the book would be attacked." What does *attacked* mean in that sentence?

8. Why did people attack her book?

9. How did Rachel Carson's book affect us all?

10. Why is the world a better place because of Rachel Carson?

Coming Clean About Toxic Pollution

Toxic Waste

Toxic waste spoils everything. It infects. It destroys. It destroys our land. It destroys our water. People dump poison. It gets into rivers. It gets into lakes. It even gets buried! Landfills are infected. Our land is damaged in
5   other ways, too. Chemicals are sprayed. Pesticides get into the air. They get into the soil. It rains. The poison drains. It runs into rivers and lakes. It runs into oceans. **Toxins** are in the air. They are in the water. We are at risk. Our animals are at risk. Our land is at risk.

Air Pollution

10   What happens when the air is polluted? We breathe in poison. We can't always see the **pollution**. Sometimes, it hangs over a city. We can see a dirty mist. This mist is smog. Smog can cover a city. **Fumes** are harmful, too. They come from cars and trucks. They can
15   make smog. Some cars have a special **device**. It changes poisons into less harmful gases. This cuts air pollution by 90 percent.

toxins
poisonous substances

pollution
contamination by harmful substances

fumes
unhealthy gases or smoke

device
a mechanical invention

Emissions from power plants react with sunlight and moisture to create acid rain.

Acid Rain

acid rain

rain that contains acid

How is **acid rain** created? It is created by exhaust. Gases come from factories. Gases come from power 20 plants. Gases come from road vehicles. These gases react with sunlight. They react with air moisture. What is the result? They produce acid rain. When acid rain falls, it causes damage. It harms everything it touches. Poison levels in soil rise. Trees lose their leaves. Plants die. 25 Statues are eaten away. In the lakes, fish die.

River Pollution

How do rivers get polluted? There are toxins in our homes. What are the sources? Paint thinner. Cleaning supplies. Bug spray. Fertilizer. All of these contain toxins. Some toxins are washed down the drain. These toxins 30 get into the sewers. They get into the soil. Then, the rain comes. The rain flushes out the toxins. Toxins wind up in rivers. There, they harm the fish.

Sea Pollution

Some plants dump chemicals. Where are they dumped? Some dump them into rivers. The poison

35 flows downstream. It pours into the sea. Small fish
feed on it. Small fish are eaten by bigger fish. Ocean
mammals eat the bigger fish. What happens? The
toxins poison the ocean. They destroy its life.

Dead Lakes

Toxins kill lakes. Farmers use fertilizers. They use
40 huge amounts. Fertilizer is important. It increases
their harvest. However, much is washed away. It gets
into streams and lakes. This causes water plants, like
algae, to grow in large numbers. This blocks out light.
It uses up all the water's **oxygen**. Fish and other water
45 animals need oxygen. There is not enough to support
them. They die.

oxygen
a gas necessary
for the survival of
living things

Your Responsibility

What is going to happen? What can you do? Can
you help? What will you do?

Answer It
Say the answer in a complete sentence.

1. How does toxic waste spoil everything?

2. How do pesticides destroy our land?

3. What happens when the air is polluted?

4. How is acid rain created?

5. How does acid rain harm the environment?

6. Where do toxins come from?

7. How is smog made?

8. How do chemicals get into our rivers?

9. How are toxins poisoning the oceans?

10. How do fertilizers cause an oxygen shortage in streams and lakes?

Riddle of the Frogs

deformed

disfigured,
misshapen

In August 1995, some Minnesota students were on a field trip. The trip was part of their science class. They had taken a nature walk. They saw some weird frogs. Some had **deformed** legs. Some had just one hind
5 leg. At first the students thought they had stepped on these frogs. They thought they had hurt them. Then they saw frogs with three or more hind legs. One frog had two feet on one of its hind legs. More than half the frogs the students found were deformed!

10 The students had taken notebooks. They recorded what they saw. They came back and took pictures. They began to ask why. They asked about bug sprays. They
fertilizers

substances that
increase plant
production

asked about **fertilizers**. They contacted scientists. They wrote to the Minnesota Pollution Control Agency.
15 They had started something. The Minnesota New Country School Frog Project had begun!

Scientists began looking at frogs, too. In many places, the same problem was found. Deformed frogs were found in Oregon, Delaware, Canada—all over.
20 Something was very wrong. But what had caused the problems? The hunt was on. The students continued to work. Now they were helping scientists. The scientists

taught them. The students learned to keep records of
the frogs. They learned to test water. The work they
25 did helped the scientists.

The students were proud of their work. They knew
that it was important. What if they had not been so
alert? What if they had not **discovered** the deformed
frogs? One student said, "If you try . . . you can make a
30 difference in your town, your city, or even your country."

Today, science has proven that toxins are dangerous.
Today, we have laws that **ban** dangerous toxins. Still,
there is much to learn. The discovery raised questions.
Other things may have harmed the frogs as well.
35 Scientists and students have lots more to do!

Rachel Carson would have been proud of these
students. Like Rachel, these students understood.
All live creatures depend upon each other. Our
environment depends on all of us. These students
40 understood that even nature's smallest creatures can
alert us. They can warn us of dangers. Danger in the
environment can affect us all.

alert
1. keenly attentive, observant
2. to warn, notify

discovered
learned through observation; realized

ban
to forbid or prohibit

environment
everything that surrounds and affects the lives of living things

Adapted from "The Riddle of the Frogs" by Judy Rosenbaum

Think About It

1. When and where did the students find the strange-looking frogs?

2. What was strange about the frogs the students saw?

3. What was the name of the project that began as the result of the students' observations?

4. The students found deformed frogs on their field trip. What other types of animals could have been affected by toxins in the environment? Why?

5. One student said, "If you try . . . you can make a difference in your town, your city, or even your country." What are some ways that you can help preserve the environment?

6. Why do you think these students were proud of their work? Why did they think their work was important?

AMAZON Toxins

Schultes and Makuna boys take shelter at the falls of Yayacopi, Río Apaporis.

Do you study plants? Can you note the differences? Are you interested in learning about them? Are you interested in old ways of healing? Do you collect leaves and flowers? Do you press them between the pages of
5   a book?

Richard Schultes did all of these things. Then, in 1941, he went to South America. He went to the country of Colombia. There, he saw a tiny orchid. He picked it and pressed it between the pages of his
10 passport. It was the first plant he collected. He would collect 25,000 more!

Richard Schultes looked for arrow and dart toxins. He went to the northwest **Amazon** area. His goal? To identify plants used to make toxins. These were known
15 as *curare* (kyōō-rä'rā). Richard looked for the best toxin makers in the Amazon—the Kofan people. The Kofan lived a **primitive** lifestyle. But they knew more than anybody else about Amazon toxins.

Richard was sure of one thing. To learn about
20 Amazon toxins, he had to understand the Kofan people. In the Kofan language, *medicine* and *poison* are the same word. *Poison* means "death to an animal." *Medicine* means "death to a disease."

Amazon
a rain forest in South America

primitive
simple, nonindustrial

Other scientists became interested. Could toxins have
value for medicine? Curare caused **paralysis**. Could it
be used to relax muscles? Could it be used in surgery?

Richard's expedition was for the National Research
Council. He was to pick curare plants. With the Kofan
medicine man, he prepared curare for study. To make
curare toxins, the Kofan use a woody vine. This vine
comes from the moonseed family. They scrape off the
bark. Then, they pour water over it and collect the
drippings. They boil the drippings. Then, they remove
the scum. Last, they apply it to the tips of darts and
arrows. Richard learned that all the Kofan know the
differences between plants. Every Kofan has his own
curare recipes. There are different recipes for each
animal and bird.

To preserve plant specimens, Schultes invented a
new method. In the old method, **specimens** were dried
with heat. A leaf dried with heat becomes **brittle**. In
his new method, specimens were dipped in alcohol
or formaldehyde. Then, they were laid between sheets
of paper.

paralysis
inability to move
one's body parts

specimens
individual items in
a group; samples

brittle
easily breakable

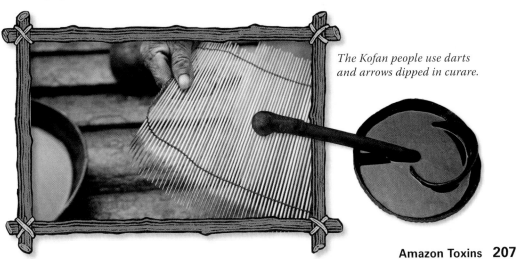

*The Kofan people use darts
and arrows dipped in curare.*

malaria

an infectious
disease spread by
mosquitoes

45   Richard Schultes risked his own safety and health. He
took risks for the sake of science. He suffered repeated
attacks of **malaria** . He was often hospitalized. He even
came down with beriberi, from a lack of vitamins.

    Today, the Amazon rain forest is shrinking. Native
50 cultures are disappearing. Now more than ever, science
needs to rescue plants. The Amazon people know the
mysteries and powers of plants. We don't want to lose
that knowledge!

    With new technology in medicine, "nature
55 becomes more important, not less important." This
is the conclusion of Mark J. Plotkin. Mark works
for the Amazon Conservation Team in Arlington,
Virginia. "Finding new and useful plants is the key to
understanding."

60   The history of Amazonian toxins is still being
written. Could you be its next explorer?

Adapted from "Hunting for Poisons" by Bernice E. Magee

Think About It

1. Where did Richard Schultes go in 1941?

2. What is *curare* (ky o͞o-rä'rä)?

3. Schultes improved upon the old method of preserving
plant specimens. Describe the difference between the old
and the new methods of preservation.

4. Why do you think that people like Richard Schultes
are willing to risk their lives for science? Think of other
professions that involve risking one's own life. Are you
interested in any of those professions?

5. Richard Schultes came down with beriberi as a result of
not getting enough vitamins. Why do you think he had
difficulty getting enough vitamins?

6. The Amazon rain forest is shrinking because the land is
being cleared for other uses. How do you think Schultes
felt about this? Why?

English Consonant Chart

(Note the voiceless/voiced consonant phoneme pairs)

Mouth Position

Type of Consonant Sound	Bilabial (lips)	Labiodental (lips/teeth)	Dental (tongue between teeth)	Alveolar (tongue behind teeth)	Palatal (roof of mouth)	Velar (back of mouth)	Glottal (throat)
Stops	/p/ /b/			/t/ /d/		/k/ /g/	
Fricatives		/f/ /v/	/th/ /th/	/s/ /z/	/sh/ /zh/		/h/[1]
Affricatives					/ch/ /j/		
Nasals	/m/			/n/		/ng/	
Lateral				/l/			
Semivowels	/ʰw/ /w/[2]			/r/	/y/		

1 Classed as a fricative on the basis of acoustic effect. It is like a vowel without voice.

2 /ʰw/ and /w/ are velar as well as bilabial, as the back of the tongue is raised as it is for /u/.

Adapted with permission from Bolinger, D. 1975. *Aspects of Language* (2nd ed.). Harcourt Brace Jovanovich, p. 41.

English Vowel Chart

ē		
1. me		
2. these		
3. see		
4. eat		
5. chief		
6. happy		
7. key		
8. either		

ĭ	
1. sit	
2. gym	

ā
1. baby
2. make
3. rain
4. play
5. eight
6. vein
7. they
8. great
9. straight

ĕ
1. pet
2. head

ă
1. cat

ī
1. item
2. time
3. pie
4. my
5. right

ŏ
1. fox
2. swap

ŭ
1. cup
2. cover
3. flood
4. tough
5. among

aw
1. saw
2. pause
3. call
4. dog
5. wall

e
1. about
2. lesson
3. elect
4. definition
5. circus

ō
1. go
2. vote
3. boat
4. show
5. toe

ŏŏ
1. took
2. put
3. could

ōō
1. moo
2. ruby
3. tube
4. chew
5. blue
6. suit
7. soup

er
her
fur
sir

ar
cart

or
sport

oi	oy
oil	boy

ou	ow
out	cow

Note: The order of spelling examples reflects the relative frequency of incidence for that spelling of the phoneme.

Vowel Chart based on Moats, L.C. (2003). *LETRS: Language Essentials for Teachers of Reading and Spelling*, Module 2 (p. 98). Adapted with permission of the author. All rights reserved. Published by Sopris West Educational Services.

Consonants

p	pup, rapped, pie	zh	vision, treasure, azure
b	bob, ebb, brother	h	hat, here, hope
t	tire, jumped, hurt	ch	church, match, beach
d	deed, mad, filed	j	judge, enjoy, jell
k	cat, kick, cut	m	mop
g	get, gill, magazine	n	not
f	fluff, rough, photo	ng	sing
v	valve, every, eleven	l	land
th	thin, three, math		
<u>th</u>	this, there, mother	w	with, wagon, west
s	sod, city, list	r	ramp
z	zebra, has, bees	y	yard, yes, yellow
sh	ship, sugar, machine		

Vowels

ē	beet	(bēt)	ō	boat	(bōt)
ĭ	bit	(bĭt)	o͝o	put	(po͝ot)
ā	bait	(bāt)	o͞o	boot	(bo͞ot)
ĕ	bet	(bĕt)	oi	boil	(boil)
ă	bat	(băt)	ou	pout	(pout)
ī	bite	(bīt)	î	peer	(pîr)
ŏ	pot	(pŏt)	â	bear	(bâr)
ô	bought	(bôt)	ä	par	(pär)
ŭ	but	(bŭt)	ô	bore	(bôr)
ə	rabbit	(ră' bət)	û	pearl	(pûrl)

a	backtrack	bond	cliff	dam
ab	bad	boss	clinic	damp
abstract	bag	box	clip	did
act	bam	brag	clock	dig
ad	ban	bran	clog	dill
add	band	brand	clot	dim
admit	bandit	brass	cob	din
aft	bask	brat	cod	dip
alp	bass	brick	coffin	disk
am	bat	brim	cog	do
amp	be	brisk	combat	dock
an	bib	cab	comic	does
and	bid	cabin	comic strip	dog
ant	big	camp	con	dog tag
are	bill	can	cop	doll
as	bin	candid	cosmic	don
ascot	bit	cannot	cost	dot
ask	blab	cap	cot	down
asp	black	cast	crab	drab
at	bland	cat	crack	draft
attic	blast	catnip	craft	drag
ax	blip	clack	cram	drastic
axis	bliss	clam	crib	drift
back	blitz	clamp	crisp	drill
backdrop	block	clap	crisscross	drip
backhand	blond	clasp	critic	drop
backlog	blot	class	crop	fabric
backpack	bobbin	classic	cross	fact
backstop	bobcat	click	dad	fad

fan	frantic	grand	hip	jog
fast	frill	granddad	his	jot
fat	frisk	grandstand	hiss	kick
fax	frizz	grant	hit	kid
fib	frock	grasp	hock	kidnap
fig	frog	grass	hog	kill
fill	frolic	grid	hop	kin
film	from	grill	hot	kiss
fin	frond	grim	hotbox	kit
fist	frost	grin	hotdog	lab
fit	gab	grip	how	lack
fix	gap	grit	I	lag
fizz	gas	habit	if	lamp
flab	gift	had	ill	land
flag	gill	ham	imp	lap
flap	give	hand	impact	lapdog
flat	glad	handbag	in	last
flax	gland	handbill	inhibit	lax
flick	glass	has	inn	lick
flint	glib	hat	intrinsic	lid
flip	glint	hatbox	is	lift
flit	glob	have	it	limit
flock	gloss	he	jack	limp
flop	goblin	her	jackpot	lint
floss	gobs	here	jag	lip
fog	golf	hid	jam	lisp
fond	got	hill	jazz	list
font	grab	hilltop	jilt	lit
for	graft	him	job	live
fox	gram	hint	jock	livid

lob	mom	picnic	quill	rot
lock	mop	pig	quilt	sack
loft	moss	pigskin	quints	sad
log	nab	pill	quip	sag
loss	nag	pin	quit	said
lost	nap	pip	quiz	sand
lot	napkin	pit	rabbit	sandbag
mad	nick	plan	rabid	sandblast
man	nip	plant	rack	sandbox
manic	nix	plastic	raft	sap
mantis	nod	plod	rag	sat
map	nonfat	plop	ram	sax
mascot	not	plot	ramp	scab
mask	now	pod	ran	scalp
mast	odd	pond	rant	scam
mat	of	pop	rap	scan
me	off	pot	rapid	scat
milk	on	pox	rat	scrap
mill	opt	prim	rib	script
mimic	pack	primp	rid	she
mint	pact	print	rift	sick
misfit	pad	prod	rig	sift
mishap	pal	profit	rim	silk
miss	pan	prom	rip	sill
mist	panic	prompt	risk	silt
mitt	pant	prop	rob	sin
mix	pass	quack	robin	sip
mob	past	quick	rock	sit
mock	pat	quicksand	rod	six
mod	pick	quid	romp	skid

skill

skim

skim milk

skimp

skin

skinflint

skip

skit

slab

slack

slam

slant

slap

slapstick

slat

slick

slid

slim

slip

slit

slop

slot

smack

smock

smog

snack

snag

snap

sniff

snip

snit

snob

sob

sock

sod

soft

sox

span

spat

spill

spin

spot

sprint

stab

stack

staff

stamp

stand

stat

static

stick

stiff

still

stilt

stock

stockings

stomp

stop

strand

strap

strict

strip

swift

swim

tab

tack

tact

tactic

tag

tan

tap

task

tax

that

the

there

these

they

this

those

tick

tidbit

till

tilt

timid

tin

tint

tip

to

tonic

top

topic

toss

toxic

toxin

toxins

track

tract

traffic

tramp

transit

transmit

trap

trick

trig

trill

trim

trip

trod

tropic

trot

twig

twin

twist

valid

valve

van

vast

vat

victim

visit

vivid

wag

was

wax

we

were

what

when

where

who

why

wick

wig

will

wilt

win

wind

windmill

wisp

wit

yak

yam

yap

you

your

zap

zigzag

zip

The definitions that accompany the readings relate to the context of the readings. They are provided to help students understand the specific reading selection. For complete definitions of these words, consult a dictionary. Pronunciations are taken from *American Heritage® Dictionary of the English Language*, Fourth Edition.

abstraction (ăb-străk'shən)— an artistic piece that doesn't look like the real object

acid rain (ăs'ĭd rān')—rain that contains acid

affects (ə-fĕks')—causes a change in; influences

agency (ā'jən-sē)—a government department in charge of certain laws and regulations

aghast (ə-găst')—shocked, horrified

alert (ə-lûrt')—1. keenly attentive, observant 2. to warn, notify

Amazon (ăm'ə-zŏn')—a rain forest in South America

associated (ə-sō'shē-ā'tĭd)—related, connected

astronauts (ăs'trə-nôts')—people trained for space flight

aware (ə-wâr')—watchful, conscious of

ban (băn)—to forbid or prohibit

barren (băr'ən)—without plant life; unproductive

bat colonies (băt' kŏl'ə-nēz)—large groups of bats living together

bold (bōld)—1. noticeably darkened 2. easily seen; flashy

borders (bôr'dərz)—dividing lines between specific areas

brilliant (brĭl'yənt)—extremely bright, radiant

brittle (brĭt'l)—easily breakable

Broadway (brôd'wā')—famous theater district in New York City

bronchitis (brŏn-kī'tĭs)—an infection in the tubes leading to the lungs

bugle (byoo'gəl)—a trumpet-shaped horn without keys

call (kôl) **and response** (rĭ-spŏns')—a singing style where one melody is repeated by others

carriage (kăr'ĭj)—an elegant wheeled vehicle pulled by a horse

choruses (kôr'ə-sĭz)—sections of a song played repeatedly

circumnavigate (sûr'kəm-năv'ə-gāt')— to go all the way around; circle

civil engineers (sĭ'vəl ĕn'jə-nîrz')— people who design and build public bridges, highways, and other structures

Columbus (kə-lŭm'bəs)—famous Italian explorer

combat (kŏm'băt')—relating to battle

complex (kəm-plĕks')—complicated, intricate

constellation (kŏn'stə-lā'shən)—a group or pattern of stars

continent (kŏn'tə-nənt)—a major landmass

control (kən-trōl')—to stop the spread of; suppress

criticize (krĭt'ĭ-sīz')—to find faults or flaws in

culture (kŭl'chər)—the language, customs, and beliefs of a group of people

debris (də-brē')—scattered wreckage, rubble

deformed (dĭ-fôrmd')—disfigured, misshapen

deliberately (dĭ-lĭb'ər-ĭt-lē)—on purpose, intentionally

desert (dĕz'ərt)—a dry region with little rainfall

devastated (dĕv'ə-stā'tĭd)—extremely upset

device (dĭ-vīs')—a mechanical invention

disbanded (dĭs-bănd'ĭd)—stopped functioning as a group; broke up

discovered (dĭ-skŭv'ərd)—learned through observation; realized

distinct (dĭ-stĭngkt')—clearly different; individual

dragons (drăg'ənz)—mythical, winged monsters

emerges (ĭ-mûr'jĭz)—comes out of; appears

environment (ĕn-vī'rən-mənt)—everything that surrounds and affects the lives of living things

eroded (ĭ-rōd'ĭd)—worn away

exaggerated (ĭg-ză'jə-rā'tĭd)—overstated or magnified

famous (fā'məs)—having widespread recognition

fertilizers (fûr'tə-lī'zərz)—substances that increase plant production

fossils (fŏs'əlz)—remains of ancient creatures embedded in the earth's crust

foundations (foun-dā'shənz)—supportive bases on which buildings stand

fragile (frăj'əl)—easily damaged; delicate

frail (frāl)—weak, sickly

frontier (frŭn-tîr')—an undeveloped area of exploration

fumes (fyo͞omz)—unhealthy gases or smoke

honored (ŏn'ərd)—respected, admired

Iceland (īs'lənd)—an island nation in the North Atlantic

ignorance (ĭg'nə-rənts)—state of being uninformed or unaware

immortal (ĭ-môr'tl)—not destined to die; eternal

improvisation (ĭm'-prŏ'vĭ-zā'shən)—creating music as it is being played

indicated (ĭn'dĭ-kā'tĭd)—served as a sign of something; showed

inspires (ĭn-spī'ərz')—causes or provokes

interfere (ĭn'tər-fîr')—to hinder or disrupt; impede

intriguing (ĭn-trē'gĭng)—very interesting; fascinating

key (kē)—a table of information on a map

lakes (lāks)—large bodies of still water

landfill (lănd'fĭl')—a site where dirt has filled in low-lying ground

legendary (lĕ'jən-dĕr'ē)—extremely well-known; mythical

limits (lĭ'mĭts)—weaknesses or shortcomings

llama (lä'mə)—a domesticated animal related to the camel

log (lŏg)—1. to record in writing 2. a data record

malaria (mə-lâr'ē-ə)—an infectious disease spread by mosquitoes

mammals (măm'əlz)—warm-blooded animals

Mardi Gras (mär'dē grä')—a holiday marked by parades and carnivals

merchant (mûr'chənt)—a person who buys and sells things for a living

mesas (mā'səz)—wide, flat-topped hills

mood (mo͞od)—the feeling or impression created

mortal (môr'tl)—destined to eventually die

negligence (nĕg'lĭ-jəns)—habitual carelessness or irresponsibility

New Orleans (no͞o' ôr-lənz')—a city of southeast Louisiana

Niger (nī'jər)—a country of west-central Africa

nominations (nŏm'ə-nā'shənz)—recommendations for awards or honors

Norway (nôr'wā')—a country of Northern Europe

opera (ŏ'pər-ə)—a performance where the story is set to music

orchestra (ôr'kĭ-strə)—a large group of musicians playing different instruments

overhaul (ō'vər-hôl')—a large repair job; renovation

oxygen (ŏk'sĭ-jən)—a gas necessary for the survival of living things

paralysis (pə-răl'ĭ-sĭs)—inability to move one's body parts

perished (pĕr'ĭsht)—died in an untimely or violent way

piano (pē-ă'nō)—a large musical instrument with a keyboard

plains (plānz)—large, flat, treeless areas of land

plantations (plăn-tā'shənz)—large farms or estates

poets (pō'ĭts)—writers of verse

pollinate (pŏl'ə-nāt')—to transfer pollen to fertilize seeds

pollution (pə-lo͞o'shən)—contamination by harmful substances

ponds (pŏndz)—small bodies of still water

porous (pôr'əs)—having many small holes or pores

predicted (prĭ-dĭk'tĭd)—said in advance; foretold

prefer (prĭ-fûr')—to choose or select a more desirable option

primitive (prĭ'mə-tĭv)—simple, non-industrial

prized (prīzd)—treasured, valued

prolific (prə-lĭf'ĭk)—having large amounts; abundant

prosperity (prŏ-spĕr'ĭ-tē)—financial success

protect (prə-tĕkt')—to keep safe

realized (rē'ə-līzd')—came to understand; sensed

recipe (rĕs'ə-pē')—the directions and ingredients to make something; a formula

remarkable (rĭ-mär'kə-bəl)—notable, extraordinary

rhythm (rĭ'thəm)—a uniform pattern of colors, lines, and shapes

rivers (rĭ'vərz)—large streams of flowing water

satellites (săt'l-īts')—information-gathering spacecraft

sediment (sĕd'ə-mənt)—a dirt-like substance consisting of tiny pieces of rock

shrines (shrīnz)—sacred or spiritual places

sneer (snîr)—a disrespectful smile; smirk

sonar (sō'när')—use of sound waves to locate objects; echolocation

specimens (spĕs'ə-mənz)—individual items in a group; samples

stars (stärz)—heavenly bodies seen as points of light in the night sky

stern (stûrn)—grim, uninviting

strikes (strīks)—failure to hit pitched balls

surveys (sûr'vāz')— studies of land features using special tools and formulas

telegram (tĕl'ĭ-grăm')—a message sent by a code-making machine

telepathic (tĕl'ə-păth'ĭk)—communication without using senses

tenor saxophone (tĕn'ər săk'sə-fōn')—a wind instrument that plays a lower range of notes

thoroughfares (thûr'ō-fârz')—main roads or streets

toxins (tŏk'sĭnz)—poisonous substances

uncomfortable (ŭn-kŭmf'-tər-bəl)—feeling discomfort

vast (văst)—very large, immense

virtue (vûr'choō)—moral excellence, goodness

vivid (vĭv'ĭd)—realistic, graphic

waifs (wāfs)—abandoned children; orphans

Grammar and Usage References

Noun Form and Function (Units 1, 2, 3, and 4)

Form	Function
Adding the suffix **-s** to a singular noun . . . . makes a plural noun.	
• map + s = maps • cab + s = cabs • mast + s = masts	• I had the **maps** at camp. • The **cabs** are fast. • The bats sat on the **masts**.
Adding the suffix **'s** to a singular noun . . . . makes a possessive singular noun.	
• Stan + 's = Stan's • van + 's = van's • man + 's = man's	• **Stan's** stamps are at camp. • The **van's** mat is flat. • The **man's** plan is to get clams.

Verb Form and Function (Unit 4)

Form	Function
Adding the suffix **-s** to most verbs . . . . makes the verb third person singular present tense.	
• sit + s = sits • skid + s = skids • pack + s = packs	• The rabbit **sits** in the grass. • The cab **skids** on the ramp. • She **packs** her bags for the trip.

Verb Form and Function (Units 5 and 6)

Form	Function
Adding the suffix **-ing** to verbs and placing a helping verb "am," "is," or "are" in front	makes the present progressive.
Unit 5: (**-ing** added to words ending with -<u>ck</u>, -<u>ff</u>, -<u>ll</u>, -<u>ss</u>, -<u>zz</u>, and final consonant blends) • pack + ing = packing • pass + ing = passing • stack + ing = stacking • plant + ing= planting **Unit 6:** (Doubling Rule) • sip + ing = sipping • skid + ing = skidding	**Unit 5:** • You **are packing** their bags for the trip. • The cab **is passing** the van in traffic. • I **am stacking** the blocks. • They **are planting** grass. **Unit 6:** • She **is sipping** milk. • The cabs **are skidding** on the damp ramp.

Subject Pronouns (Unit 4)

Person	Singular	Plural
First Person	I	we
Second Person	you	you
Third Person	he, she, it	they

The Present Tense (Unit 4)

Person	Singular	Plural
First Person	I sit.	We sit.
Second Person	You sit.	You sit.
Third Person	He, she, it sits.	They sit.

The Present Progressive (Unit 6)

Person	Singular	Plural
First Person	I am sitting.	We are sitting.
Second Person	You are sitting.	You are sitting.
Third Person	He, she, it is sitting	They are sitting.

Prepositions (Unit 4)

about	at	during	of	toward
above	before	except	off	under
across	behind	for	on	until
after	below	from	over	up
against	beside	in	past	with
along	between	inside	since	
among	beyond	into	than	
around	by	like	through	
as	down	near	to	

Idioms

Idioms (Units 4 and 5)

Idiom	Meaning
at the drop of a hat	immediately and without urging
be in the swim	active in the general current of affairs
be in the wind	likely to occur; in the offing
be on the rack	be under great stress
be on to	be aware of or have information about
do the trick	bring about the desired result
fill the bill	serve a particular purpose
hit the jackpot	win; have success
hit the sack	go to bed
hit the spot	be exactly right; be refreshing
kick the habit	free oneself from addiction, as cigarettes
pass the hat	take up a collection of money
pat on the back	congratulate; encourage someone
stick to your ribs	be substantial or filling; used with food
tilt at windmills	confront and engage in conflict with an imagined opponent or threat

Book A contains these terms. Unit numbers where these terms first appear follow each definition.

Adjective. A word used to describe a noun. An adjective tells which one, how many, or what kind. A prepositional phrase may also be used as an adjective. Example: *The* **quick** *team* **from the school** *won the game.* (Unit 6)

Adverb. A word used to describe a verb, an adjective, or another adverb. An adverb answers the questions when, where, or how. A prepositional phrase may also be used as an adverb. Examples: *He ran* **daily**. *She hopped* **in the grass**. *He batted* **quickly**. (Unit 4)

Antonym. A word that means the opposite of another word. Examples: *good/bad; fast/slow; happy/sad* (Unit 2)

Apostrophe. A punctuation mark that shows singular possession. Examples: *Sam's hat* (the hat that belongs to Sam); *Fran's stamps* (the stamps that belong to Fran). (Unit 2)

Attribute. A characteristic or quality, such as size, part, color, or function. Examples: *She lost the* **big** *stamp. Fish have* **gills**. *He has a* **green** *truck. A clock* **tells time**. (Unit 5)

Comma. A punctuation mark used to signal a pause when reading or writing to clarify meaning. Examples: *Due to snow, school was cancelled. At the end, the class clapped.* (Unit 5)

Compound word. A word made up of two or more smaller words. Examples: *backdrop, hilltop, jackpot, bigwig* (Unit 3)

Consonant. A closed sound that restricts or closes the airflow, using the lips, teeth, or tongue. Letters represent consonant sounds. Examples: <u>m</u>, <u>s</u>, <u>t</u>, <u>b</u> (Unit 1)

Direct object. A noun or pronoun that receives the action of the main verb in the predicate. Answers the question: Who or what received the action? Examples: *Casey hit the* **ball**. *She dropped* **it**. (Unit 3)

Doubling rule. A spelling rule in English that says to double a final consonant before adding a suffix beginning with a vowel when it's (1) a one-syllable word, (2) with one vowel, and (3) ends in one consonant. Examples: *hopping, slipping, robbing*. Also called the 1-1-1 Rule. (Unit 6)

Expository text. Text that provides information and includes a topic. Facts and examples support the topic. Example: "What Is Jazz?" (Unit 5)

Idiom. A common phrase that cannot be understood by the meanings of its separate words— only by the entire phrase. It cannot be changed, or the idiom loses its meaning. Example: at the drop of a hat = immediately and without urging (Unit 4)

Narrative text. Text that tells a story. A story has characters, setting, events, and a resolution. Example: "Atlas: The Book of Maps" (Unit 2)

Noun. A word that names a person, place, thing, or idea. Examples: *teacher, city, bat, peace* (Unit 1)

Noun, abstract. A word that names an idea or a thought that we cannot see or touch. Examples: *love, Saturday, sports, democracy* (Unit 3)

Noun, common. A word that names a general person, place, or thing. Examples: *man, city, statue* (Unit 3)

Noun, concrete. A word that names a person, place, or thing that we can see or touch. Examples: *teacher, city, pencil* (Unit 3)

Noun, proper. A word that names a specific person, place, or thing. Examples: *Mr. West, Boston, Statue of Liberty* (Unit 3)

Phrase. A group of words that does the same job as a single word. Examples: *at lunch, in the park, to stay in shape* (Unit 4)

Plural. A term that means more than one. In English, nouns are usually made plural by adding -**s**. Examples: *figs, backpacks, quilts* (Unit 1)

Possession, singular. One person or thing that owns something. Adding **'s** to a noun signals singular possession. Examples: *The man's map, Fran's stamps* (Unit 2)

Predicate. One of two main parts of an English sentence. It contains the main verb of the sentence. Examples: *He **digs**. She **lost the big stamp**.* (Unit 2)

Preposition. An English function word that begins a prepositional phrase. Examples: *at, in, from* (Unit 4)

Prepositional phrase. A phrase that begins with a preposition and ends with a noun or a pronoun. A prepositional phrase is used either as an adjective or as an adverb. Examples: *at the track, in traffic, from her* (Unit 4)

Progressive, present. A verb form that indicates ongoing action in time. The **-ing** ending on a main verb used with **am**, **is**, or **are** signals the present progressive. Examples: *I **am going**. She **is visiting**. We **are trying**.* (Unit 5)

Pronoun. A function word used in place of a noun. Nominative (subject) pronouns take the place of the subject noun in a sentence. Examples: *I, you, he, she, it, we, you, they* (Unit 4). Objective pronouns take the place of the object of a preposition, a direct object, or an indirect object. Examples: *me, you, him, her, it, us, them* (Unit 6)

Sentence. A group of words that has a subject and a predicate. A sentence conveys a complete thought. Examples: *It kicks. The map is in the cab.* (Unit 1)

Sentence, simple. A group of words that has one subject and one predicate. Examples: *The man ran. The plan is abstract.* (Unit 2)

Statement. A sentence that presents a fact or opinion. Examples: *The map is flat. The twins are remarkable.* (Unit 1)

Story. An account of events. A story has characters, a setting, events, and a resolution. Example: "Floki: Sailor Without a Map" (Unit 2)

Subject. One of two main parts of an English sentence. The subject names the person, place, or thing that the sentence is about. Examples: ***She** raps. **Boston** digs. **The machine** printed a map.* (Unit 2)

Syllable. A word or word part that has one vowel sound. Examples: *bat, dig, pic-nic, tox-ic* (Unit 3)

Synonym. A word that has the same meaning as or a similar meaning to another word. Examples: *big/huge; quick/fast; fix/repair* (Unit 3)

Tense, present. A verb that shows action that is happening now. The **-s** at the end of a verb signals present tense. Examples: *he hops, she drops, it stops* (Unit 4)

Verb. A word that describes an action *(run, make)* or a state of being *(is, were)* and shows time. Examples: *acts* (present tense; happening now), *is dropping,* (present progressive; ongoing action), *acted* (past tense; happened in the past), *will act* (future tense; will happen in the future). (Units 1, 4, 5)

Vowel. An open sound that keeps the airflow open. Letters represent vowel sounds. Examples: **a**, **e**, **i**, **o**, **u** and sometimes **y** (Unit 1)

Sources

Unit 1

At Bat

Hechtkopf, Jacqueline. 2002. "At Bat," from *Cricket* (August), vol. 29, no. 12. Reprinted by permission of *Cricket* magazine, August 2002, vol. 29, no. 12. Text © 2002 by Jacqueline Hechtkopf.

Bats in China

Kern, Stephen J. 1988. "Bats in Chinese Art." *Bats*, vol. 6, no. 4. Austin, TX: Bat Conservation International, Inc.

Batty About Bats!

Kowalski, Kathiann M. 1999. "Batty About Bats!" from *Odyssey* (March 1999), vol. 8, no. 3. Carus Publishing Company, 315 Fifth Street, Peru, IL 61354. All rights reserved. Adapted with permission.

Casey at the Bat!

Found on Patrick McGovern's website, "The Baseball Scorecard," www.baseballscorecard.com/casey1.htm. March 2, 2003.

Unit 2

Atlas: A Book of Maps

Rosenbaum, Judy. 1999. "The Story of Atlas," from *AppleSeeds* (January), vol. 1, no. 5. Carus Publishing Company, 315 Fifth Street, Peru, IL 61354. All rights reserved. Adapted with permission.

Floki: Sailor Without a Map, a Norse Myth

Rosinsky, Natalie M. 1999. "Here Be Dragons," from *AppleSeeds* (January), vol. 1, no. 5. Carus Publishing Company, 315 Fifth Street, Peru, IL 61354. All rights reserved. Used with permission.

The Hardest Maps to Make

Kushner, Sherrill. 1999. "Oceans: Mapping Earth's Last Frontier," from *AppleSeeds* (January), vol. 1, no. 5. Carus Publishing Company, 315 Fifth Street, Peru, IL 61354. All rights reserved. Used with permission.

A Map Is a Sandwich

Miller, Jeanne. 1999. "A Map Is a Sandwich," from *AppleSeeds* (January), vol. 1, no. 5. Carus Publishing Company, 315 Fifth Street, Peru, IL 61354. All rights reserved. Adapted with permission.

Mapping the Unknown

Rosinsky, Natalie M. 1999. "Here Be Dragons," from *AppleSeeds* (January), vol. 1, no. 5. Carus Publishing Company, 315 Fifth Street, Peru, IL 61354. All rights reserved. Used with permission.

Microsoft® Encarta® Online Encyclopedia. 2003. "Dragon," encarta.msn.com © 1997–2003 Microsoft Corporation. All rights reserved.

Unit 3

Africa Digs

Laliberte, Michelle. 2000. "Finding the Pieces...and Putting Them Back Together Again," from *Odyssey* (September), vol. 9, no. 6. Carus Publishing Company, 315 Fifth Street, Peru, IL 61354. All rights reserved. Adapted with permission.

The Big Dig

Toupin, Laurie Ann. 2002. "Big Dig," from *Odyssey* (September), vol. 11, no. 6. Carus Publishing Company, 315 Fifth Street, Peru, IL 61354. All rights reserved. Adapted with permission.

Dig This!

Kornegay, Shureice. 2000. "Fantastic Journeys: Dig This!" from *Odyssey* (September), vol. 9, no. 6. Carus Publishing Company, 315 Fifth Street, Peru, IL 61354. All rights reserved. Adapted with permission.

Unit 4

Conjoined Twins

Chichester, Page. 1995. "A Hyphenated Life," *Blue Ridge Country*, (November/December), blueridgecountry.com/newtwins/twins.html.

Tankala, Varun. *Conjoined Twins*, www.conjoined-twins.i-p.com.

Gemini: The Twins

Peoria Astronomical Society. 2002. "Gemini," www.astronomical.org/constellations/gem.html.

Raasch, Rick. 1998. "The Constellation Gemini: The Twin Brothers," *The Constellation Home Page*, ed. Edward P. Flasphoehler Jr., The American Association of Amateur Astronomers, www.corvus.com/con-page/winter/gem-01.htm.

Remarkable Twins

Dunn, Marcia. 1999. "As Pilot Prepares to Fly, His Double Helps Out, But Doesn't Step In." STS-103, *Houston Chronicle*'s Space Chronicle (May 2), www.chron.com/content/interactive/space/missions/sts-103/stories/990502.html.

Elvis Presley Enterprises, Inc. 2003. "All About Elvis," biography from Elvis Presley: The Official Website, www.elvis.com/elvisology/bio.

Sanders, Craig. 1999; 2003. "Twin Portraits: Twins in Outer Space," Twinstuff.com (April; February), www.twinstuff.com/twinnasa.htm.

———. 1999. "Twin Portraits: The Twin Wranglers," Twinstuff.com (May), www.twinstuff.com/wranglers.htm.

Twin Towers: Two Perspectives

BBC News. 2001. "The Twin Towers Fall." (Tuesday, 11 September), news.bbc.co.uk/2/hi/Americas/1574550.stm. (Accessed January 23, 2004)

Sanders, Craig. 2001. "Twin Powers: A Twin's Thoughts on the World Trade Center's Twin Towers," Twinstuff.com (Oct. 8), www.twinstuff.com/twinpowers.html.

Unit 5

The Duke Jazzes Newport

Miller, Brandon Marie. 1993. "Making a Statement at Newport," from *Cobblestone* (May), vol. 14, no. 5. Carus Publishing Company, 315 Fifth Street, Peru, IL 61354. All rights reserved. Adapted with permission.

Growing Up With Jazz

Gelber, Carol. 1994. "Growing Up with Jazz," from *Cobblestone* (October), vol. 15, no. 8. Carus Publishing Company, 315 Fifth Street, Peru, IL 61354. All rights reserved. Adapted with permission.

Spatz, Virginia A. 1994. "Scat and Improvisation," from *Cobblestone* (October), vol. 15, no. 8. Carus Publishing Company, 315 Fifth Street, Peru, IL 61354. All rights reserved. Adapted with permission.

Jazz: The Recipe

Amey, Heather Mitchell. 1983. "Jazz Ingredients," from *Cobblestone* (October), vol. 4, no. 10. Carus Publishing Company, 315 Fifth Street, Peru, IL 61354. All rights reserved. Adapted with permission.

Looking at Jazz

Miller, Marc H. 1994. "Looking at Jazz," from *Cobblestone* (October), vol. 15, no. 8. Carus Publishing Company, 315 Fifth Street, Peru, IL 61354. All rights reserved. Adapted with permission.

Unit 6

Amazon Toxins

Magee, Bernice E. 2001. "Hunting for Poisons," from *AppleSeeds* (April), vol. 3, no. 8. Carus Publishing Company, 315 Fifth Street, Peru, IL 61354. All rights reserved. Adapted with permission.

Coming Clean About Toxic Pollution

Wadsworth, Virginia Evarts. 1989. "Cleaner Cleaning," from *Cobblestone* (August), vol. 10, no. 8. Carus Publishing Company, 315 Fifth Street, Peru, IL 61354. All rights reserved. Used with permission.

Marsh, James. 1995. "Yuck! It's Time to Come Clean About Pollution," from *Young Telegraph: Earth Alert*. Chanhassen, MN: Two-Can Publishing Ltd. © Two-Can Publishing, an imprint of Creative Publishing International, Inc., 1995, all rights reserved.

Rachel Carson

Salsbury, Sylvia. 1999. "Rachel Carson's World of Wonder," from *AppleSeeds* (March), vol. 1, no. 7. Carus Publishing Company, 315 Fifth Street, Peru, IL 61354. All rights reserved. Adapted with permission.

Riddle of the Frogs

Rosenbaum, Judy. 1999. "The Riddle of the Frogs," from *AppleSeeds* (March), vol. 1, no. 7. Carus Publishing Company, 315 Fifth Street, Peru, IL 61354. All rights reserved. Adapted with permission.

Photo and Illustration Credits

Unit 1

Photographs

1: Mark Kostich. 26–27: ©Merlin D. Tuttle, Bat Conservation International. 29: ©William O'Conner, Denver Art Museum. 31: ©National Baseball Library/MLB Photos. 34: ©Digital Vision.

Illustrations

10–25: Rick Stromoski. 32: Marty Peterson.

Unit 2

Photographs

71: ©Royalty Free/Corbis.

Illustrations

44–59: Jack Hornady. 60: ©Eureka Cartography LW. 63: ©Woods Hole Oceanographic Institution. 65: ©North Winds Picture Archive. 67: ©North Winds Picture Archive. 68: ©2004 Cobblestone Publishing Company, illustrated by Craig Spearing. 72: ©North Winds Picture Archives.

Unit 3

Photographs

73: ©Corbis Images/PictureQuest. 100: ©Paul S. Sereno, courtesy Project Exploration. 101: ©Paul C. Sereno, courtesy Project Exploration. 102: ©Project Exploration. 103: ©1999–2003 Getty Images. 104: *bkgd.* courtesy of Massachusetts Turnpike Authority Central Artery/Tunnel Project; *t.* ©PhotoDisc. 105: courtesy of Massachusetts Turnpike Authority Central Artery/Tunnel Project. 106: *t.* courtesy of Massachusetts Turnpike Authority Central Artery/Tunnel Project; *b.* courtesy of Massachusetts

Turnpike Authority Central Artery/Tunnel Project. 107: ©Gabrielle Lyon, courtesy Project Exploration. 108: ©Paul C. Sereno, courtesy Project Exploration. 110: ©PhotoDisc.

Illustrations

84–99: Steve McGarry.

Unit 4

Photographs

111: *t.l.* ©Royalty Free/Corbis; *t.r.* Jan Coy; *m.l.* Mark Doliner; *m.r.* ©Getty Images; *b.l.* Barbara Page; *b.r.* ©Creatas. 125: ©Used by permission, Elvis Presley Enterprises, Inc. 134: ©Used by permission, Elvis Presley Enterprises, Inc. 135: ©Artville 136: *bkgd.* ©Digital Stock; *b.l. & b.r.* courtesy of National Aeronautics and Space Administration. 138: *bkgd.* ©Digital Stock. 144: ©1999-2004 Getty Images. 141: Courtesy of North Carolina Collection, University of North Carolina Library at Chapel Hill. 146: ©Steve Spak/ 911 Pictures.

Illustrations

129: ©New York Public Library, Spencer Collection. 131: Rick Geary. 140: Pauline Brown.

Unit 5

Photographs

171: ©Lisette Model Estate: National Portrait Gallery, Smithsonian Institution/ Art Resource, NY. 172: ©Louis Armstrong House & Archives at Queens College/ CUNY. 175: ©Louis Armstrong House & Archives at Queens College/CUNY.

Illustrations

147: Martin French. 161: ©Getty Images. 163: ©Getty Images. 166: ©Getty Images. 169: "Hot Still Scape for Six Colors—Seventh Avenue Style" by Stuart Davis ©2004 Museum of Fine Arts Boston. 176: Susan Jerde.

Unit 6

Photographs

179: ©Royalty Free/Corbis. 191: Shirley A. Briggs, courtesy of Lear/Carson Archive. 193: ©George Silk/Time Life Pictures/Getty Images. 195: ©Royalty Free/Corbis. 196: ©Royalty Free/Corbis. 198: Shirley A. Briggs, courtesy of Lear/Carson Archive. 199: ©Frances Collins/Beinecke Rare Book and Manuscript Library. 201: ©Dynamic Graphics. 202: ©Getty Images. 206: R.E. Schultes. 207: ©Alison Wright/Corbis.

Illustrations

204–205: Ursula Vernon. 206–208: Ursula Vernon.